Peter Maggs grew up in Ealing in West London. He left school with one 'O' level and spent several years playing rock 'n' roll with various bands. Following a spell of conventional work and night school, he studied Physics at university, and followed a career in the engineering industry. He developed an interest in nineteenth-century social history through investigations into the genealogy of his family, and took early retirement to spend more time doing research. *Murder in the Red Barn* is his third book. He has also contributed articles on genealogy to various magazines.

# Murder in the Red Barn

*The tragic story of*
*Maria Martin and William Corder*

By Peter Maggs

Published by Mirli Books, 2015

© Peter Maggs 2015


Published in the UK by
Mirli Books Ltd,
21 Highfield Road
Chelmsford CM1 2NF
www.mirlibooks.com


ISBN 978-0-9562870-2-1


A catalogue record for this book
is available from the British Library


Reprinted 2016


Also by Peter Maggs:
*Henry's Trials*
*Smethurst's Luck*


Design: Gill England
Print: MBC Print Consultancy

I dedicate this book to the memory of Professor Alan F Gibson FRS, gifted physicist and educator, in whose cottage in Polstead I first heard tell of Beauty Smith and his alleged involvement in the Red Barn Murder.

*Unhappy man! Though you at first conceal*
*Your perjuries, yet punishment at last*
*Creeps on with silent feet.*

Tibullus, Elegies

## Acknowledgements

Sincere thanks are due to staff at Bury St Edmunds Record Office who could hardly have been more friendly, helpful and supportive during my frequent visits in support of this new investigation into the Red Barn affair. Grateful acknowledgement is also made of staff at the British Library, National Archives, Middle Temple Library, Norwich Record Office and the National Library of Australia. Thanks are due to Essex Libraries for their continuing provision of online access to millions of pages of nineteenth-century newspapers and other resources.

Once more Diane Hardy has demonstrated astonishing attention to detail in disentangling the farrago of incorrectly spelled names, wayward hyphens, excessive ellipses and general lack of order and coherence that was the draft version of this book. I am most grateful to Shane McCorristine for locating a note in the press on the death of William Corder's son in 1892, and to Jackie Nesbitt for an inspired suggestion of the origin of 'Beauty' Smith's name. My wife Jacky has never failed to support me in my research and writing, and as ever, provides my backstop in questions of style, spelling and grammar.

# Contents

# Introduction

In 1972 I was living in Wivenhoe, an attractive village on the river Colne just a short distance from Essex University where I was a postgraduate student. If Wivenhoe is known to the world at large, it is probably because of John Constable's beautiful picture, *Wivenhoe Park*, which is in the National Gallery of Art, Washington DC; Wivenhoe Park is now the home of Essex University. One of my housemates, Sarah, had been helping in a house clearance. She came across an old book which she thought might interest me. The book, *"An Authentic History of Maria Marten or The Red Barn"*, had no accredited author.* I dipped into it and was interested, not the least reason for which was that the murder, for murder it was, had been committed in Polstead, Suffolk, where my academic supervisor lived. But more than that, the murderer, William Corder, had been arrested in Brentford, next door to Ealing in West London. I grew up in Ealing and went to school in Brentford; I must have passed the place where he was arrested a thousand times.

The murder in the Red Barn captured the public imagination. The story had all the elements of a Gothic novel; the victim was a comely maid, daughter of the village mole-catcher, seduced by William Corder, the dissolute son of a prosperous local farmer. She went to rendezvous with him in the Red Barn dressed in male clothing to avoid being identified, prior to them both going to Ipswich ostensibly to be married. In the barn he shot her, possibly stabbing her also, and buried her body under the floor. Corder then told her father that they

---

* It was a bootlegged copy of the celebrated book on the case by J Curtis.

were happily married and Maria was unable to write to him because of a bad hand. He, meanwhile, moved to London where he advertised for a wife, married a lady, and settled down in a girls' school run by his new wife in Brentford. The deed was discovered after Maria's stepmother dreamed that Maria had been murdered and buried in the Red Barn. Her father probed the floor with his mole-spike and found the body.

From the time that Maria's body was discovered in April 1828, until the August, when William Corder was hanged for her murder, the story was a sensation. The press had blanket coverage; there were peepshows, puppet shows and broadsheets, and a Nonconformist minister preached a sermon at the Red Barn attended by thousands. Stage dramas were written and produced – latterly in films and on television – and the story of Maria Martin has continued to be written about until the present day.

But there remain some perplexing questions regarding Maria's murder and the subsequent discovery of her body. The most intriguing of these is the way the body was discovered – after Maria's stepmother dreamed that she had been done to death and buried in the Red Barn. At the time, this explanation was accepted largely without question, and after William Corder was hanged, *The Times* ran a story recounting another 'astounding case' where a person had dreamed of an event that was subsequently found to be true. These days such an occurrence would be regarded with profound suspicion. Three surgeons concluded that Maria had not only been shot, but stabbed in several places with a sharp instrument and possibly strangled. Yet Corder in his confession, hours before his execution, admitted that although he did indeed shoot Maria and bury her body, he denied vehemently ever having stabbed her.

Having spent some years researching and writing up two relatively unknown legal cases from the mid-nineteenth century, I found myself drawn back to the tale of Maria Martin.

The story of the Red Barn murder has been told on numerous occasions; many accounts can be found in compendia of true-life crime as well as books entirely devoted to the subject. Of the latter, at least six have been published since 1949, and I fully expected to find very little remaining to be said about the affair. In fact much of what has been written about the actual events seems only to succeed in confusing established fact with hearsay, old wives' tales, fantasy and, it must be said, deliberate falsehood. One account makes the most sensational allegations about the murder, claiming that it was a conspiracy involving several people. Such of those claims that can be checked, have been impossible to verify and several have been proven to be false. Another author confuses what is documented fact with a fictional account published soon after the event. There is, in my view, a pressing need to set the record straight.

There is another reason why a new account of the murder is justified now. Over the last five to ten years the number of resources available to the social historian has grown at an astonishing rate, due mainly to the burgeoning quantity – and quality – of historical records that can be interrogated via the Internet. It is now possible to do word-searches on several million pages of nineteenth-century newspapers and journals and detect information that otherwise would have been virtually impossible to find. The Mormon Church has produced a peerless set of records, made freely available to everyone, providing wider than ever coverage of births, marriages and deaths from the eighteenth and nineteenth centuries and earlier. A number of commercial websites have exploited the enormous upsurge in interest in genealogy and made available prodigious amounts of information, all searchable via the Internet. It is, therefore, possible that some new facts may be gleaned to add to the small number of primary sources of information on the Red Barn murder. Several authors have taken as read, so-called facts reproduced in previous accounts, some of which have taken great liberties with the historical

11

record. It is appropriate, therefore, to construct a narrative based strictly on what is known from verifiable sources, and try to understand what really happened on that late spring day nearly two hundred years ago in Polstead.

## *A Note on the Text*

This account of a new investigation into the Red Barn affair is intended to be an accessible narrative based on verifiable sources, rather than a rigorous academic study. However, since major criticisms are made of previous books on the subject, notably those of McCormick and Haining – see Appendix 4 – no authority for the veracity of any new history can be claimed unless references to declared facts are very clearly indicated. This presents the writer with a dilemma, in that readability and flow are inevitably compromised if the reader has to constantly turn to references elsewhere in the book. Details of William and Maria's lives are taken mainly from J Curtis's book and Charles Hyatt's published sermon, both published in 1828 – see Appendix 3 – and these form the basis of the sequence of events. Where facts are not directly referenced, they have been taken from these two sources and will not be individually noted other than by comments in the text like 'Curtis claims' or 'Hyatt says' etc. Information is also freely reproduced from the many press reports about the case, and this is used to augment material from Curtis and Hyatt. Details of births, marriages and deaths, unless otherwise stated, are taken from the appropriate parish registers. The original and correct spelling of Maria's surname, *Martin*, rather than *Marten*, has been used in this new account – see Appendix 3 for an explanation.

Press reports and other information will be referenced in the text with a number and collected at the end of the book, ordered by chapter. Where a clarification that would impede the narrative flow is needed, it will be flagged and shown at the bottom of the page. Direct quotations from sources, generally retaining the original spelling and punctuation, are indicated either by quotation marks, or by indenting the text; where these lack a capitalized first word or full stop at the end, only part of a sentence has been reproduced. References to the *Oxford Dictionary of National Biography*, are noted *ODNB*, and to the *Oxford English Dictionary*, *OED*; online editions of the *ODNB* and *OED*, 2014 & 2015, were consulted.

# Prologue

England in the late 1820s; the Duke of Wellington, victor at Waterloo, was Prime Minister, and there had been a King George on the throne for more than 100 years – the current monarch was the fourth of that name. George IV's father had lost the American colonies, but with the defeat of Napoleon, Britain entered a golden age of expansion; peoples from the Canadian provinces in the west, to Africa, the Middle East, India, the Far East and Australia would owe allegiance to the British Crown. The Industrial Revolution was in full swing at home; the world's first public railway had opened between Stockton and Darlington in 1825, and employment in factories and other industrial enterprises had, for a number of years, exceeded the numbers working on the land and in fisheries. In England the population was nudging 13 million, of whom just three percent were able to vote in parliamentary elections. Slavery was still legal in the British Empire.

Life in rural England though continued much as it had done since the Norman Conquest and before. When Maria Martin's body was discovered buried in the Red Barn at Polstead in April 1828, the village was virtually unknown. Within days it was on everyone's lips as gruesome details of the murder began to emerge. Polstead, deep in the heart of Suffolk with its life steeped in agriculture, must hardly have noticed the Industrial Revolution. Domesday Book, 1086 AD, mentions Polstead, in the hundred of Babergh, Suffolk, as having fifty-two households; the population had grown to around 900 by 1828. The church dates from around 1160 AD and the parish registers were started in 1538. There was a Gospel Oak in the grounds of Polstead Hall; according to tradition, St Cedd, the Saxon Missionary who came to Essex in 653 AD, was said to have preached under it.[1] Polstead's previous claim to fame seems to have been its cherries, and the village held an annual Cherry Fair on the 16 and 17 July; the 'Polstead Black' was unsurpassed:

> the ripe fruit is black and of a refined and exceptional flavour which no-one has succeeded in reproducing elsewhere[2]

But it would be wrong to think that the village was a rural idyll. Waterloo had been won, but the workforce was glutted with servicemen demobilized from the army and navy. Together with bad harvests and a substantial rise in the birth rate, an intolerable strain was placed on the agrarian economy:

> The worst years for labourers were those after 1815 … Wages fell by about a third between 1814 and 1822 while southern labourers often faced entire winters of dependence on charity and Poor Law allowances.[3]

Grievances exploded in the South East and East Anglia in 1830 with the Swing Riots. Hayricks were burnt and threshing machines destroyed. Polstead was not immune:

> Suffolk – Three stables, barns and a coach house were consumed by fire on Tuesday [22 December 1830] at Polstead belonging to Mr B Smith, farmer and liquor merchant. A large quantity of agricultural implements were at the same time wholly destroyed.[4]

Polstead had occasionally found itself in the newspapers before this, but usually as the dwelling place of bankrupts and miscreants, with the occasional sales notice and list of approved gamekeepers. The Red Barn murder was to change all that; the village would never be the same again.

# Maria Martin

Maria Martin was the daughter of Thomas Martin, the Polstead mole-catcher. Thomas's stated occupation when he gave evidence in William Corder's trial was 'labourer and mole-catcher'. Many mole-catchers were itinerant workers, there not being a sufficient regenerating population of moles in any one area to occupy a man full time; mole-catchers tended to move around to different regions where their speciality was needed. Thomas must have combined his mole-catching with general labouring for which there was always a need in any rural farming area, and from his efforts he was able to rent a five-roomed cottage in Polstead. He was only 22 years old in 1793 when he married 25-year-old Grace Willis; if he did not bring his new wife to the cottage immediately after their marriage, he was certainly occupying it by 1801 when Maria was born there. Thomas Martin must have been a hard worker and prudent with money.

Grace bore Thomas five children; Maria was their second child and eldest daughter, born on 23 July 1801. At an 'early age' Maria was sent to help in the nursery of a clergyman at Layham, a parish adjacent to Polstead. Curtis says she was recalled by her father when her mother died in 1811; elsewhere it was reported that Maria was dismissed through 'levity of behaviour'.[1] In any event, she returned home and the following year her father remarried. Thomas's new wife was Ann Holder or Holden, 21 years his junior; she came from Groton, also adjacent to Polstead, and she bore him three more children.

Maria was, it was said, very fond of her father, and always spoke of her dead mother with affection. The Martins' cottage had a garden with cherry trees and roses front and back, some of which were planted by Maria and tended by her. She was, in her seventeenth year,

> Possessed ... of no ordinary personal advantages ... a handsome face, a fine form and figure ... a superior address ... and a modest demeanour

Her 'superior address', or manner of speaking, was a consequence, no doubt, of living with a clergyman and his family for some time. In addition to that it was said that Maria was not given to the habit of 'walking out' like other girls, preferring to attend to her domestic duties. Unlike her mother, she had learned to read and write and according to Peter Mathews, one of her subsequent paramours, she could write very well.[2]

It all changed though when she was 18. Having obtained information from 'unquestionable sources', Curtis assured his readers that Maria's first seducer, her 'base destroyer', the man who caused her to lose that 'inestimable pearl', was Thomas Corder, one of William Corder's older brothers. Thomas would have had to pass the Martins' cottage on farm business, and must have become acquainted with Maria as a result. Whether he really was her first seducer is impossible to know, but she became pregnant two years later, and Thomas Corder was acknowledged to be the father. The child, Matilda Martin, was baptized in June 1822 but died three months later. Curtis reported that Thomas Corder conducted the affair in strict secrecy due to their disparity in station, and his visits grew less frequent after Maria became pregnant. She did not go to a magistrate for a bastardy order, because, it was said, she was still in hope of a permanent connection to Thomas. He did though provide the minimum support such an order would have demanded during Maria's 'accouchement', and afterwards, until the child died.

If Curtis is to be believed, even while Maria was pregnant with Thomas Corder's child, a 'gentleman of great respectability' was making overtures to her; so respectable was he that Curtis forbore to mention his name. The gentleman, Peter Mathews, renewed his attentions later on and Maria responded, egged on by her 'playful and vivacious disposition, and a mind naturally sanguine ... perhaps ambitious.' That Maria did respond is evidenced by the birth in December 1824 of their son Thomas Henry Martin. Maria was 23, Peter Mathews was 38. Whether Mathews had an occupation or was just a 'gentleman' is unclear. His address was given variously as 'Clement's Inn', and Binfield, near Wokingham, Berkshire. Clement's Inn was an 'Inn of Chancery, appertaining to the Inner Temple'[3], but Peter Mathews does not appear in any of the Law Lists of the period, so he may just have had London apartments in the road called Clement's Inn, close to the Temple. He was certainly there during the 1851 census, living at No 14.

Mathews was the son of Richard and Ann Mathews of Binfield, Berkshire; he was the youngest of nine children, of which five survived to adulthood. At the time of the Red Barn affair, his eldest brother, John Staverton Mathews, was rector of Hitcham, a parish a few miles north of Polstead, and his sister, Mary Ann, had married Thomas William Cooke of Polstead Hall. Thomas Cooke was Lord of the Manor of Bildeston, five miles or so north of Polstead, where his father had been the rector. Peter Mathews thus had reason to come to the Polstead area and visit his brother and sister (nine and ten years respectively his elder). He may not have been his father's favourite son; when Richard Mathews first made his will, leaving £2,000 each to Peter's brothers and sisters, Peter was left just fifty pounds to mourn his father, he having 'given [him] substantial sums from time to time'. Evidently he relented, because in a codicil Richard Mathews left his son an estate in Newington

Butts (Southwark), together with one sixth of the residue of his estate after the various bequests had been settled. Whatever the value was of that estate, and whether or not Peter Mathews was a shrewd investor or businessman, when he died in 1870 he left £18,000, a considerable sum worth more than £800,000 in today's money.[4]

From Maria's perspective, Peter Mathews must have been able to provide her with what she and many other young women then craved for, fine clothes and courtly attention. In her evidence given during Corder's trial, Maria's stepmother, Ann Martin, said that she (Mrs Martin), Maria's sister, Ann Martin junior*, and Thomas Martin used to quarrel with Maria about her clothes. They were remarkably fine clothes for the daughter of a farm labourer; the Prosecution Brief lists what Maria took with her on her final visit to the Red Barn: a Leghorn† hat trimmed with black 'ribbands', a black silk gown, a black cambric skirt, a silk shawl, two pairs of shoes (apart from the ones she was wearing), a black silk handkerchief, a pair of white kid gloves, a black silk veil and two pairs of black silk stockings together with some 'lawn' pocket handkerchiefs. She also had a green cotton umbrella.

Peter Mathews did the half-decent thing by Maria – since marriage was impossible – and settled five pounds per quarter on her to support their child. It was a generous amount, four times what the parish of Assington, adjacent to Polstead, demanded at the time from the father of an illegitimate child for support.[5] Mathews sent the money, via the post office, as a five-pound note. According to evidence he gave during the murder trial, Mathews claimed that he had last seen Maria on 31 August 1826, eighteen months after Thomas Henry was born. There was no explanation of why the liaison was cut short; perhaps it was terminated by Maria on the realization

---

* Ann Martin junior was six years younger than Maria, and her full sister.

† This was a hat made of 'fine plaited straw' from *Leghorn* (= Livorno in Italy), from where the straw was imported (*OED*).

that even with the baby, Mathews was not going to marry her. Their stations were entirely different: Peter Mathews was the son of a very rich landowner, with a brother who was rector of a local parish and a sister married to the occupant of Polstead Hall, another very rich landowner and the Corders' landlord to boot. The rector of Hitcham cannot have been very happy that his brother was conducting an affair with a farm labourer's daughter in a nearby parish. Thomas Cooke was also unlikely to be thrilled with the knowledge of his brother-in-law's illicit relationship. Possibly it was upheavals in Mathews' own family that caused the break-up; Thomas Cooke died in July 1825, and Richard Mathews, Peter Mathews' father, died in early 1826.

According to all of the evidence, it was in 1826 that Maria became intimately acquainted with William Corder. It is not difficult to understand how they knew each other. William would have known about her liaison with his brother and he may have been acquainted socially with Peter Mathews – he certainly knew him later. Like his brother, William had cause to pass the Martins' cottage on farm work. William and Maria were certainly lovers by the early summer of 1826.[*]

Maria Martin was no blushing virgin, but was she really the 'whore of Polstead' as implied by one of the witness statements and repeated by at least one subsequent commentator? It is impossible to assess with any confidence the level of 'illicit' sexual activity in a rural village in the 1820s, but there is one indicator that cannot lie. Between 1813 and 1837 the Polstead baptismal register recorded 798 baptisms, of which thirty-five were illegitimate births. Of course there is not a direct correlation between recorded extramarital births and extramarital sex, but one thing is clear, the former cannot happen without the latter. Maria Martin's name appears twice in these records[†], but of the thirty-five such births recorded,

---

[*]   Their child was born the following March or April

[†]   The child she had with William Corder was never baptized

Sara Porley also had two children, Elizabeth Deaves and Elizabeth Humphrey each had three, and Sarah Stow produced no less than four. Thus Maria was barely a runner-up in the illegitimate children stakes.[6]

# *William Corder*

J ohn Corder was a tenant farmer in Polstead farming around 300 acres of land rented from Thomas Cooke at Polstead Hall. According to Curtis, Corder was

> a respectable yeoman of the old school ... not only industrious, but rigidly economical.

At the time of his death, he was a relatively wealthy man. In March 1792, when he was around 30 years old, John Corder married 25-year-old Mary Baalham in Polstead. In view of the subsequent libidinous behaviour of three of his sons, it is perhaps appropriate to mention that Mary Baalham was around four months pregnant with her first child when she was married. Since that marriage was by licence, not a cheap option for the normally parsimonious Corder, it might be inferred that it was a fairly hurried affair initiated as soon as her condition became known.[1]

According to the parish records the Corders had ten children between 1792 and 1807. Three died in infancy, one, Hannah, died at the age of 15; four sons and two daughters survived to adulthood. William Corder was born on Midsummer's day, 21 June 1804, the ninth child and second youngest of the four boys. His eldest sister, Mary, married a local miller, Jeremiah Borham in 1813; all of his other siblings were single, he and his brothers being engaged in working on the farm. John Corder junior had his own farm, and almost certainly lived separately. The other sister, Elizabeth, lived at home with her mother. The family occupied a substantial timber-framed house in the centre of the village close to Polstead Hall, and the Red Barn was part of the Corders' farm.

Different sources attribute the origin of the name, 'Red Barn', variously to its actual colour[2], the red tiles used to roof one of its bays[3] and the 'reddish hue it had on the evening of a splendid sunset'.[4] Curtis observed sniffily:

> one of the ephemeral publications which arose out of this transaction, gravely informs us, that "it seems to have taken its name from the tiles that cover part of it;" and, "because a chaff-house which is a lean to against it, and a wagon shed, at some *little distance* from it, are covered with tiles."

He continued,

> The truth is, that no part of the barn, of which we have given a faithful representation, is covered with tiles – its entire roof being of thatch.

And this is a little confusing, because his 'faithful representation' clearly shows an apparent lean-to quite obviously roofed with tiles. Nevertheless, Curtis insisted that the name derived from the fact that the barn was originally coloured red, and a conservation leaflet published by the St Edmundsbury Borough Council states:

> Up to the late 17th century, barns were generally plastered. An alternative covering from that time until the present day was clapboarding, often in elm, which was either left natural or painted red.[5]

The paint was probably linseed oil with red ochre added to inhibit the growth of mould and moss. The 'reddish hue at sunset' explanation, since it seems to derive from McCormick, can probably be discounted; the Red Barn was called as such because it was, or had been, painted red.

It is of interest to try and establish something of William Corder's character, and therein lies a difficulty. Much has been written about him, but contemporary accounts are difficult to trust in their objectivity, given that the behaviour of a convicted murderer was being described. Curtis spent two weeks in Polstead in July 1828 talking to the locals, many of whom knew Corder personally; his account must, therefore, have some credence. The other substantial source of information is Charles Hyatt's sermon. What follows is condensed mainly from Curtis's descriptions and Hyatt's sermon; there is some confusion regarding the order of events, but the essentials of William's life are probably correct.

William Corder attended the village school at Polstead until he was 13 or 14, at which point he was sent to a boarding school at Hadleigh where he spent several years.[*] One of his schoolfellows claimed that he was addicted to lying, and could 'lie like the truth'; on account of this he was nicknamed 'Foxy'.[†] The name suggests cunning, which implies deceit or evasion, but also cleverness and ingenuity. Corder certainly used the two former in his stories explaining Maria Martin's apparent disappearance, but some of the other things he did following her death would seem to betray rather limited intelligence, not to say extreme stupidity.

Following his return from school at the age of 16 or so, Corder spent some years helping his father and brothers run the farm. He was described as being five feet four inches tall, slender, and with a tendency to stoop forward when walking, holding his left hand, Napoleon-style, at his breast. He was fair and freckled but had poor eyesight, '[being] obliged to put a book very near [his eyes] in order to read its contents'. In spite of this, it was claimed, he was an excellent shot with a pistol.

---

[*] Curtis said Corder spent five years at the school in Hadleigh.

[†] Curtis spelled it 'Foxey'

In conversation, it was said, he did not 'express ... himself with frankness'.

William Corder was not a favourite with his father, although his mother was very attached to him. Perhaps in consequence of his father's disapprobation, rather than trying to please, William embarked on a number of petty frauds against him, usually detected, which must have served only to further blacken his character in his parent's eyes. On one occasion he borrowed a ten-pound note, in his father's name, from one of his acquaintances. When, after some time, that gentleman approached his father for repayment, the fraud was discovered. William's father observed that he 'did not know what to do with the boy'; he did make a comment to the effect that the money William took would be deducted from any future inheritance. On another occasion William sold some pigs belonging to his father to a neighbour. When this was found out, his father bought them back, paying the neighbour what he had paid William. According to Curtis, this last event exhausted Corder senior's patience, and he determined that William would go to sea. He was sent to London to pursue this plan, but no ship's captain would accept him on account of his poor eyesight. Other plans to 'expatriate' him proved abortive and he returned to Polstead.

At some point Corder became acquainted with a girl from the village whom Hyatt named only as H. She would 'accompany him into the fields', where 'as the wages of her iniquity', he would load her up with peas from his father's crops. The identity of H is naturally intriguing, and a report of Hyatt's sermon in the *Essex Herald* named the girl as *Hazell*. The newspaper described her as a 'very loose character' of 'about Corder's age'. From the context it is clear that Hazell was her surname; the use of 'Hazel' as a first name was, in any case, very unusual until the end of the nineteenth century.[6] On 18 May 1806, Sarah Hazell was born to Thomas and Mary Hazell in Polstead. At some point they moved to Assington, the parish adjoining Polstead to the west, and there, on 8 November 1824, Sarah gave birth to a child, Meshack Glass, out of wedlock.[7] The alleged father was James Glass, a footman from Dedham. Such a proceeding would certainly qualify Sarah Hazell for the title 'very loose character', and she fits the description of William Corder's lover, H. If Hyatt's sequence of events is correct, William preceded James Glass in Sarah's affections.

After a while, Hyatt says, H went to London to work as a prostitute, and Corder took up with another girl, unnamed, who had a child by him that died while he was in Bury gaol; Curtis does not mention this girl or her child. Corder was a frequent visitor to public houses, being free with his money although he was not a great drinker, his sobriety being one of his few reported virtues. And in a curious juxtaposition of 'vices': 'He kept the lowest company [and] resorted to bell-ringing as a diversion'. Hyatt claimed that Corder would also attend 'fairs and revels' miles from home, and sometimes persuaded an old schoolmate to accompany him, Corder paying the expenses. Once they went to a 'bad house and stopt [sic] all night'; money was obtained by defrauding his father. William's association with women was not a unique family trait; as has already been noted, his own father had impregnated his mother well before they were married. His brother Thomas had produced an illegitimate child with Maria Martin, and on 16 May 1822, a bastardy order was made against John Corder junior, William's eldest brother, by Hannah Snell.[8] John Corder Snell was baptized on 21 April 1822 at the local workhouse, the Cosford House of Industry, at Semer, a few miles north of Polstead.

Then a sort of Damascene conversion took place. According to Hyatt, the occasion was the ordination of Benjamin Moore on 7 April 1824, at the Boxford Independent meeting house. Charles Hyatt was Benjamin Moore's pastor, and, as it happened, six days later, Hyatt's daughter, Elizabeth, married Moore at St Dunstan's Stepney. Foxy Corder came to witness the 'solemn and interesting proceedings' at Boxford, and a strong impression having been made, he immediately broke off from his 'companions and vicious habits'. He was just under 20 years old. He started reading the Bible and stayed at home on Sundays to read to his 'aged' parents. Corder's mother told Hyatt that her 'most wicked son' now seemed to be her 'best boy'. There was a report in the newspapers, Hyatt said, that Corder had preached a sermon at a meeting in Polstead. This was not correct, although he had 'given out a hymn' at the meeting. Hyatt met Corder, he said, at the house of a mutual friend in Hadleigh. Corder was at pains to tell him of the opposition of his parents, who were church people, i.e. Anglicans, to his attendance at a 'dissenting place of worship'. Hyatt insists that he urged Corder to see to his farm duties, even though it was the Sabbath day. With hindsight, Hyatt said, Corder was probably not telling the truth.

In July 1825, it all changed again. It was the occasion of the annual Polstead fair, and the girl H, with whom Corder used to romp in the pea-fields, returned from London and was now a

> polished prostitute. Her showy appearance and insinuating manner completely ensnared him, he again commenced intimacy with her

After a few weeks, she went back to London, followed by Corder who had drawn 'a considerable sum of money in his father's name' from the bank.* According to Hyatt, H had since died 'in a most awful and miserable way'. If H was Sarah Hazell, she must have abandoned her child, and left him with his grandparents; the parish register of Assington records the burial of Meshack Glass Hazell on 17 October 1826.

---

* This journey to London may have been when Corder was supposed to be trying to get a place on board a ship. The sequence of events is not clear.

Some months later Corder came back to Polstead, possibly following the death of his father in December 1825; this would have removed the need for an immediate explanation about the embezzled money. John Corder senior made his will on 16 December 1825; he died two days later. As a measure of the regard in which he was held locally, the following notice appeared in the *Ipswich Journal* of 7 January 1826:

> On Sunday 18th ult. Died, at Polstead, after a short and painful illness, in the 64th year of his age, Mr John Corder, a respectable farmer of that place. He was a tender husband, an affectionate father, and kind friend, and was highly and deservedly respected for his integrity and upright conduct. As a very useful, active, and intelligent man he will be much missed by his fellow parishioners, and his death be sincerely regretted.

He was buried on 24 December and the will was proved on 9 June 1826 in Norwich. Since the will was made just two days before John Corder's death, he either forgot, or realizing his end was close, forgave William his behaviour; he was treated exactly the same as the rest of the family. John Corder made his wife Mary and the two elder sons, John and Thomas, joint executors, and directed that all of his assets be turned into cash, the proceeds being equally split between his wife, the four brothers, John, Thomas, William and James, and two daughters Elizabeth Corder and Mary Borham. The total effects were 'less than £2,000', and there was a sting in the tail for Mary Borham; she had to account for £400 already advanced to her. What this meant was that John Corder's assets amounted to £2,400 split seven ways, around £350 each and Mary was required to return £50 to the testamentary pot.[9]

Possibly William's anticipated wealth from his father's legacy emboldened him. Curtis reported that in lieu of part of his inheritance he was offered a copyhold estate, but declined because he couldn't be bothered with the running of it. He confirmed his de-conversion from religion by giving away a hymnbook he had purchased, and about this time he took up with Maria Martin. There was also a report that Corder had told someone on seeing a Bible that he 'used to believe it but didn't any more', and he was to be seen around carrying a copy of Count Volney's *Ruins, Meditation on the Revolutions of Empires.*\* Hyatt commented:

> Those who know its contents will soon cease to wonder at its effects on so depraved a heart

Which shows what a humbug Hyatt was; he admitted that he had been unable to get hold of a copy of the book so he could hardly judge what it contained.

It was probably about this time that Corder was involved in a second pig stealing episode, this time with the help of one Samuel 'Beauty' Smith, a local bad character. Beauty Smith figures much later in the story, but suffice it to say that it was a mean trick, since the man they stole the pig from was not well off. 'Bill' Corder's character was deteriorating by the day.

---

\* Count de Volney was a one time member of the National Assembly at the time of the French Revolution. Among other things, his book, translated by Thomas Jefferson, sought a morality without God.

# *Those Twain*

What was it that Maria Martin and William Corder saw in each other? Both were well versed in the more sordid ways of the world; Maria had already had two illegitimate children by two different fathers, one of them William's brother. That child had died, but Peter Mathews' son was thriving, and by all accounts was a beautiful boy. From the point of view of Corder, who was in expectation of a substantial inheritance from his father's estate, Maria was just a labourer's daughter with a severely damaged reputation and no financial resources other than the annual twenty pounds she received for Thomas Henry's upkeep. But she was still handsome, with a fine figure and a 'superior address'. Also, she had a 'levity of spirit', so she was probably fun to be with. Those virtues, coupled with her liberal attitude to physical love, were, no doubt, what attracted Corder to her.

Why was Maria attracted to him? The most reliable portrait of him shows a not bad looking though diffident young man, with a turned up nose and freckles. William walked with a stoop and was described as 'short'. The post-mortem results though, reported

> as fine a display of muscular proportion and strength ... as I have ever witnessed ... The body was perfectly healthy, and every organ sound.

Maria may have thought that William's financial prospects were interesting. Possibly she was attracted by William's apparent unconventional attitude to life. He had rejected the Church, he was experienced with other girls, including the showy H, and

31

he had spent some time in London. William and Maria became lovers, using as a trysting place the Red Barn and sometimes his room at home via a private stairway. In his defence speech in court, Corder said that he and Maria spent many hours, and some nights, in the Red Barn. The inevitable happened; Maria's third child was conceived in the summer of 1826.

And then something happened that no-one could have predicted. In the cold January of 1827, Thomas Corder was unwise enough to attempt to walk across the frozen pond at Polstead to talk to Mr Chaplin who was on the other side; the pond was just a few yards from the family home. The ice broke and he fell in. Chaplin raised the alarm but it was Thomas's dead body that was recovered from the pond. This was a catastrophe for the family; since John Corder senior's death a year earlier, his son Thomas had been running the farm. John junior had his own farm and the other brother, James, was in poor health, probably suffering from consumption. Suddenly, William's prospects changed overnight. Foxy Corder, his mother's one time 'best boy', was now the only hope for the day to day management of the farm. In addition to that, with Thomas dead, William only had to share his father's inheritance with the remaining five; if James died, it would only be four.

But like a Greek tragedy, at the moment of William's triumph came the portent of his doom. Stealing a pig from a poor man was mean, but what Corder did next, was quite contemptible. Maria had been receiving five pounds per quarter from Peter Mathews in order to support their little boy; the money was sent in the form of a five-pound note. At the time, banknotes were similar to cheques today; they were partially printed, with some details entered by hand. Upon receipt of a banknote, the normal procedure was to take it to a bank and exchange it for gold sovereigns and/or silver coin, the note being endorsed by the bank with the name of the person who had presented it. Corder intercepted one of the letters from Peter Mathews containing the five-pound note, took it to the bank in Hadleigh and cashed it, pocketing the money. Maria, distressed that the money had not arrived, wrote to Peter Mathews. Mathews instituted an enquiry at the post office at Colchester to discover that

> the identical note sent by him had passed through the hands of a person named Corder.

The postmistress, Miss Savage, accompanied by a solicitor, went to the Corder's house to find out whether any of the family had knowledge of the incident. William was at home, and denied he knew anything about it. Peter Mathews went to the bank in Hadleigh, and following an interview with Mr Baker, and Mr Baker junior, members of the staff there, discovered that a young man of the name Corder had presented the note, and they, thinking it was the youngest of the Corder brothers, James, had entered his name on the note. Mr Baker junior told Mathews that the person who presented it had a 'defect of the eyes'. James Corder was asked to speak to William, who once more denied all knowledge of the affair and went to the bank to remonstrate with them in an 'extremely high and haughty manner'. However, Mr Baker junior recognized Corder as the person who had presented the note, and suggested that he should go to the post office in Colchester and 'get the matter settled as soon as possible'. This apparently he did, although to indemnify himself from any further action he persuaded Maria, from whom he had stolen the money, and now fairly heavily pregnant with his child, to write to the post office saying that she had, in fact, received the note after all. Curtis reproduced the letter, which he described as written in a 'good plain hand, and very correct in its orthography' – Maria had good handwriting and could spell:

Polstead, February 27, 1827

Madam, This is to certify, that the letter posted at Wokingham, January the 3rd, and directed To 'Thomas Marten, Polstead,' wherein was enclosed a five-pound Bank of England note, I duly received on the following Friday, January 5th.

I remain, your obedient servant, Maria Marten

To Miss Savage, Post Office, Colchester

It might be wondered why Maria was happy to perjure herself in writing in order to save William from prosecution. Evidently she took a practical view; if she hoped to get any protection or support or even marriage from William in her delicate state, standing by while he was prosecuted for theft might not further her interests. The death of Thomas Corder had improved William's prospects considerably. The incident was to rankle though, and they frequently had arguments about it as attested by Ann Martin during the trial. Peter Mathews, in order to prevent a recurrence, sent just half of a banknote on the next occasion, sending the other half only when he had had written confirmation from Maria that she had received the first part.

What conflicting emotions must have been running through William's head as he arranged to rent rooms in Sudbury[*] for Maria's confinement? Her pregnancy had been concealed from William's mother and the rest of the family, presumably from the rest of Polstead also, although according to Curtis, William had flaunted Maria around Polstead, showing her off as his lover. During Maria's time at Sudbury, William visited her two or three times a week, and Mr and Mrs Goodwin, from whom the rooms had been rented, commented

---

[*] About eight miles from Polstead.

that they appeared to be fond of each other; Mrs Goodwin did say though that Maria was frequently in 'bad spirits'. Maria had arrived in Sudbury on 19 March and left on 16 April 1827, when William brought her and the new baby back to Polstead in his gig. According to Thomas Martin, the child was 'weakly'. A few weeks later, at about nine o'clock in the evening, after Thomas had gone to bed, Maria, in tears, brought the child into her parents' bedroom saying that it was dying. Ann Martin took it in her arms and a little while later, it did die. Ann wrapped it up in some cloth and it was put into a box in the bedroom. Curtis reported that when knowledge of the baby's history came out following the inquest, there was 'considerable suspicion' in the village regarding its fate, the implication being that Corder was involved in some way in its demise. Corder denied in court that the baby's death was by 'violent means'.

According to Corder, he and Maria entered into an elaborate charade to dispose of the child's body. The birth had been concealed from the parish officers, but William and Maria pretended to take the dead baby, at night, to Sudbury to be properly interred. In fact they buried the body in the fields, and Maria was then secreted in Corder's room in his house for the following day and night before she returned home, in order to complete the illusion that she had been to Sudbury. Corder claimed that Maria's stepmother had agreed with this plan although she denied knowledge of it in court.

From William's perspective, his outlook now was most promising. His younger brother James was seriously ill; he died later in the month. His elder brother John was also not well. William was the only one left to run the farm – and pocket the profits – and if John died too, his father's money would be split only four ways. Any liability William had in respect of Maria had disappeared; there was no child to support, and since he hadn't married her, he was technically free from any encumbrance. But events were moving towards their tragic climax; William and Maria decided to get married.

They probably planned it during Maria's stay in Sudbury. Her sister, Ann Martin, commented in court on Maria's view of the relationship:

> I am not aware that my sister wanted very much to marry the prisoner, but I have heard her say that she should marry him.

From Maria's point of view William was a very good catch, even though from her sister's testimony she may have been wanting in enthusiasm for it. William's position was more problematic. He may have suspected that within a few weeks he would be the sole surviving brother; James was very ill, and his closeness to death had already delayed the proposed marriage. Since his brother John had his own farm, William was effectively in charge of the Corders' farm. What, then, at the threshold of his emergence as a man of property and importance, was the point of joining himself for life to a poor country girl with a ruined reputation, putting aside the possibility that he really was in love with her?

But Maria had a double hold over him. There was the question of the dead baby; they had concealed the birth and such a charge could, and very likely would, carry a sentence of between one and two years in prison. Far worse though was the theft of the money. William Corder did steal the five-pound note from Maria. She wrote a letter saying that she had, after all, received the money, but she could easily say that in her condition of advanced pregnancy, the letter was written under duress. There was plenty of evidence, including that of at least one eyewitness at the bank willing to swear that William had cashed the stolen note. Such an offence would have got him transportation or even the rope. Although both William and Maria were complicit in the clandestine burying of the child, the taking and cashing of the five-pound note was unquestionably down to William; had Maria wished to, she could easily have had him charged with theft. Maria's stepmother, heard them arguing frequently; she heard Maria say to Corder: 'if I go to prison, you do too'. Having said all of that, if Maria had told the authorities either about the buried child or the stolen five pound note, she would have incriminated herself and would certainly have gone to prison also. It seems possible therefore, that William and Maria decided to get married simply because they wanted to. Apart from the obvious mutual attraction, William was a 'good catch' about to inherit a prosperous farm, and Maria was a good-looking, lively, well-dressed and sensual woman.

The arrangement was that they would drive to Ipswich in William's gig and get married there. Maria's stepmother provided a commentary on what happened. On Sunday evening, 13 May 1827, Corder took Maria away with him; they were to sleep at his mother's house and then leave for Ipswich early the next morning. In the event, Maria returned home at three or four o'clock in the morning. On Monday William arrived and told Maria that they would go to Ipswich on the Wednesday. They didn't go on Wednesday; William said they would go on Thursday. Thursday was put off on account of William's brother James being close to death. James must have rallied, because William arrived around midday on Friday in a hurry, and told Maria to get ready to leave. According to Ann Martin, Maria said: 'How can I go at this time without anybody seeing me?' William had told Maria and her family that there was an order out against her for burdening the parish with bastard children, and she was to be arrested if seen. If the Martins had thought about it, they would have realized that this story was nonsense. Maria's first child was dead, so there was no liability on the parish in respect of it; Thomas Henry Martin was being supported by Peter Mathews and no-one knew about child No 3, which was, in any case, also dead. Since Maria herself was not claiming relief, there was no case to answer. Having illegitimate children was not, of itself, against the law. Corder explained the deception in court by saying that he wanted to conceal from his mother and dwindling family that he was going off with Maria to get married.

Maria was to be disguised in male clothing, supplied by William, when she left the Martins' cottage. He would take a bundle containing her clothes up to the barn, and when he came back they would walk together to the barn; 'None of my workmen are in the field,' Corder said, 'I know the coast is clear.' The plan was that Maria would change in the barn, William would bring his gig from home, and they would drive together to Ipswich. They left by different doors and met at a gate by the road; they then walked together in Hare Field towards the barn. Mrs Martin said that Maria was crying and William 'had a gun in his hand' that he told her was loaded. Elsewhere it was stated that Maria was upset because her little boy, Thomas Henry, had refused to kiss her, not recognizing his mother in male attire. Mrs Martin never saw Maria again.

Of what happened next we only have William Corder's testimony and the results of the various post-mortems on Maria's body. What is certain is that she died in the Red Barn, probably of a gunshot wound, possibly also by being stabbed or strangled. William left three different accounts of what happened; all agreed in one particular: they had a violent argument. Nessworthy has published an early draft of Corder's defence statement taken from an original handwritten copy.[1] In this account, Corder says that they argued about the dead child and the five-pound note; Maria thought him too proud to take her to his mother's house. He left her on the road to Ipswich and never saw her again; he had no idea how she met her death. In his actual defence statement, the one given in court, he said that they argued in the barn, he left her there, heard a gunshot and returned to find her on the ground and bleeding heavily. The implication was that she had shot herself. Twelve hours before his execution, William Corder made a confession in which he stated that he and Maria had been arguing, among other things, about the dead child, she insisting that its burial place would be found. There was a scuffle, he took the gun from his pocket and shot her. In his defence statement and his confession, he admitted burying Maria's body in the Red Barn, but he always denied stabbing her. He made no comment, however, on strangulation although he said that he may have dragged the body through the barn by the handkerchief around the neck.

# What William Did Next...

**M**rs Martin saw William Corder the next day at his mother's house, and then at around nine o'clock on Sunday morning, 20 May, when he came to the cottage. He told her that Maria had changed into her proper clothes and left the barn with him in his gig; they were there for no more than half or three-quarters of an hour. He had taken Maria first to Ipswich, then to stay with 'Miss Rowland', who was the sister of a school friend of his. She lived 'by the waterside'. Maria didn't need any more changes of clothes, because Miss Rowland was able to supply her with her needs. Corder had bought the marriage licence but it had to go to London for signing, so they could not get married for a month or six weeks. Maria had plenty of money because he had changed a cheque for twenty pounds. But Mrs Martin's youngest son George, aged 10, was collecting grass for his donkey on the day Maria had left, and he saw Corder later on in the afternoon, walking between the Red Barn and his house with a pickaxe over his shoulder. Ann Martin challenged Corder on this and he said that it must have been Tom Akers who was planting trees on 'Mr Hay's hill'.

William was now busy managing the Corders' farm, and soon he was the only one left to do so. His brother James succumbed to consumption days after Maria left home with William. Over the next few months, Mrs Martin saw William quite often. It being summer, there was much to do on the farm and no doubt he passed the cottage frequently. Maria was very well, he told her, staying with his friend's sister, but she was unable to write to the Martins, because she had a bad hand. Later on he told Maria's father that she did not write because she was too busy. However, William made a serious mistake at James's funeral. Mrs Martin attended the funeral, just eleven days after Maria had left, and she noticed that William had an umbrella which she knew to be Maria's by an ivory button on it and the 'crome' (hooked) handle. She asked him about it afterwards, expressing surprise that Maria had not taken it with her. He said the umbrella was similar to Maria's but actually belonged to Deborah Pryke who had forgotten it. Some months later, just before Corder left Polstead, she asked him about the umbrella again. This time he said that Maria had lent it to him because it had been raining in Ipswich.

On 14 July 1827, John Corder, William's last remaining brother died, most likely also from consumption. John willed the lease of his own farm and other assets to his mother. William was now managing his father's 300-acre farm and almost certainly his brother's farm also. William's mother was the sole executor of both her husband's and son's estates, and William was her best boy, and the only remaining male member of the family. His father's liquid assets were now to be shared between William, his mother, and his two sisters, around £600 each. His brother John's estate was worth about £450, also to be shared between William and his two sisters after their mother's death. But the storm clouds had started to gather. Peter Mathews was in Polstead in July and had an interview with William on the subject of the five-pound note that had gone missing. Initially William denied all knowledge of it but then he wrote Mathews a grovelling letter dated 1 August 1827:

Sir,

After a long and wretched night of miserable reflection, I have at last endeavoured to collect my weary spirits, in order to fulfil your request, and humbly submit you will pardon my addressing you personally on the subject, as I am at a loss for one word on my own behalf, and,

41

therefore, must depend entirely upon your merciful and generous principles, which I have already experienced in your promising to forgive the enormous crime, on condition that I would openly confess it. I will therefore, with the greatest possible humility, throw myself at your feet and implore your pardon

He went on to regret having tried to deceive Mathews with 'lies and false pretentions' adding that 'the idea of the dreadful news reaching my poor distressed mother, fills me with horror'. Evidently Mathews accepted the apology because on 26 August, Corder addressed the following letter to him:

Sir,

In reply to your generous letter, which reached me yesterday ... I was indeed ignorant of Maria Marten's residence at the time you requested me to forward the letter I took from Bramford, [a village near Ipswich] and will candidly confess that Maria have been [sic] with a distant female relation of mine since the Month of May. About five weeks ago they both went into Norfolk, to visit some of my kindred friends. On Friday week I received a letter from my kindred, who informed me that Maria was somewhat indisposed, and that they were in a village called Heringby near Yarmouth.

He went to Heringby, he said, and saw Maria who had a 'sore gathering on the back of her hand' which prevented her writing to Mr Mathews. He concluded by declaring that he would marry Maria in four to six weeks' time as soon as some family matters were settled. Mathews replied on 2 September, expressing sorrow at Maria's indisposition, and pleasure in hearing that they would soon be married. He wanted, he said, to be a friend to all, with a 'friendly feeling for your own welfare, and for the sake of your worthy mother'. He also enclosed a letter he wished to be forwarded to Maria, and requested her formal address so he could write to her directly. It is notable that no parish of 'Heringby' exists in either Norfolk or Suffolk, and no village of that name exists today, although there is reference to 'Heringby, 7 miles from Yarmouth' in a 1798 directory published by John Cary.

William Corder spent the summer working on the farm and getting in the harvest; he must also have been managing his brother John's farm since he was the only one left to do so. Perhaps the sustained physical work did not agree with him; possibly he took the view that the farm(s) could support him as a gentleman of leisure. Possibly also, he was having trouble with his conscience. According to Corder himself, he was advised by a local doctor to go to the south coast to a 'watering place' for his health; he may have been worried that he was developing the condition that killed his two brothers.[*] He decided to get someone to take over from him and manage his father's farm. His mother must have approved of this move; she of course was mourning the loss of three sons over the previous seven months and would have agreed to whatever her best boy asked for, particularly since it was apparently for his health. The person selected for the job of manager was William Pryke, who was already bailiff of the farm. It was Pryke who drove Corder to Colchester when he left Polstead; the date was 19 September. They discussed mainly farm matters, but when Maria's name was mentioned Corder said he had not seen her since May. Pryke said: 'he spake very highly of her, and said nothing more.'

A month later, on 18 October 1827, William Corder wrote to Maria's father from the Bull Inn at Leadenhall Street, London. The letter was a cruel and cynical attempt to maintain the fiction that Maria was alive and well. He had just arrived in London to transact some family business, and was writing to

---

[*] Corder's doctor confirmed, in evidence given at his trial, that he exhibited signs of consumption, and that he advised him to go to a 'warm bathing place ... on the south coast'.

catch the last post because he was 'anxious to return again to her *who is now my wife*'. He went on:

> it was her wish to stay at our lodging in Newport, in the Isle of Wight, which she described to you in her letter, and we feel astonished that you have not yet answered it

He continued:

> she gave you a full description of our marriage, and that Mr Rowland was 'daddy', and Miss, bridesmaid ... I told Maria I should write to you directly I reached London, who is very anxious to hear from you

He asked for any letters from 'Mr Peter' to be forwarded to 'Mr W C' at The Bull, and also whether Mathews had acknowledged little Thomas Henry; after a lot of extraneous padding to add credibility to his account, he suggested that Thomas should burn all the letters, 'that nobody may form the least idea of our residence'.

Thomas Martin's answer has not survived, but one may make a reasonable guess at its contents. Corder's reply was sent on 23 October. After another charade about finding out why the post office had 'lost' Maria's letter, he said:

> Were it not for the discovery of our residence, I would certainly indict the Post Office, but I cannot do that without making our appearance at a Court Martial which would be very unpleasant to us both. You wish us to come to Polstead, which we should be very happy to do, but you are not aware of the danger. You may depend that if ever we fall into Mr P's hands the consequence would prove fatal

Here is Foxy Corder in full flight. He sought to confuse Thomas Martin by talking about a 'Court Martial' which sounds terrifying, but is a tribunal which applies only to members of the armed forces. Then he invented the fiction that Peter

Mathews was after them, by implication regarding the theft of the five-pound note, and went on to advise Thomas Martin to say that they, William and Maria, had gone to foreign parts. He also advised Thomas to ask Mathews for support for young Thomas Henry. He finished by saying that the coach was about to leave, without telling Thomas Martin their address in Newport. It was a wretched piece of obfuscation, and must have left the Martins confused, anxious and upset. They never heard from Corder again.

Corder wrote another long letter on 18 October, addressed to George Gardiner at Polstead. George Gardiner seems to have been one of William Corder's few friends, although ultimately, he was his undoing. Since leaving Polstead in September, Corder told Gardiner, he had been to Portsmouth, the Isle of Wight, Southampton, Plymouth, Devonport, Exeter and Salisbury. He had spent several days with a most 'charming, innocent and lovely female' from Yorkshire going to the Isle of Wight to see a brother of hers who was in the army at Albany Barracks. More than three-quarters of the long letter was spent describing their time together. He said that he had promised to write to her but wondered whether he ever would.

In view of what Corder did next, it is odd that he did not write to the lady, who was a widow with a child and had obviously made a deep impression on him, because he advertised for a wife. The *Morning Herald* was a London newspaper which William would have been unlikely to have seen in Polstead. Perhaps it was coincidence, but the very day he arrived in London, 19 September, the newspaper printed two advertisements for wives at the top of its front page. Both were modest and unassuming; in each case, a middle-aged man with a small income was seeking a companion who possessed a similar financial independence. Three more similar advertisements for wives appeared in October, and on 13 November 1827, despite a notice the previous week: 'ADVERTISING for a WIFE, an admired Comic song, sung by

Mrs. Fitzwilliam', the *Morning Herald* published the following, reproduced in full, exactly as printed:

> **Matrimony. – A Private Gentleman, aged 24,** entirely Independent, whose disposition is not to be exceeded, has lately lost chief [sic] of his family by the hand of PROVIDENCE, which has occasioned discord amongst the remainder, under circumstances most disagreeable to relate. To any female of respectability, who would study for domestic comforts, and willing to confide her future happiness to one in every way qualified to render the marriage state desirable, as the advertiser is in affluence the Lady must have the power of some property, which may remain in her own possession. Many very happy marriages have taken place through means similar to this now resorted to, and it is hoped no one will answer this through impertinent curiosity, but should this meet the eye of any agreeable lady who feels desirous of meeting with a sociable, tender, kind, and sympathising companion, they will find this advertisement worthy of notice. Honour and secresy [sic] may be relied on. As some little security against idle applications, it is requisite that letters may be addressed (post paid) A.Z., care of Mr. Foster, stationer, 68 Leadenhall-street, with real name and address, which will meet with most respectful attention.

The advertisement was repeated, minus the comment about the lady's property, and with one extra full stop, in the *Sunday Times* of 25 November, albeit with *entirely* spelled *Intirely*, and *honour* spelled *honor*.[*] A.Z. was William Corder, and some insights into his background, character and motives are illuminated by this curious notice. It is quite clear that he

---

[*] The OED recognizes *honor* and *secresy* as old forms, but *Intirely* is entirely spurious.

had lifted a number of key phrases from elsewhere, joining them together with little understanding of sentence structure or punctuation. His limited education was quite effectively demonstrated, a fact which should have been obvious to anyone reading the item. His comments regarding discord within his family provided a convenient smokescreen to prevent embarrassing enquiries about his life and connections in Polstead. William stated that he was in affluence in order to allay any suspicion that he was a fortune-hunter; he may even have deluded himself that he really was well off, although as was to become clear within a few months, his rate of spending in his new life outstripped by many times any income he could expect from the farm. Very probably he did understand his precarious financial position.

It seems likely that his motivation for finding a wife with property was to provide him with the income that he needed; evidently the lady from Yorkshire was just not rich enough. The position and size of the advertisement in the newspaper – at the top of the front page, almost in the centre and more than three times larger than most of the adjacent notices – must have made it very expensive; possibly it was a deliberate act in order to demonstrate his 'affluence'. The insertion in the *Sunday Times* was right in the centre of the first page. It is interesting to note that the *Leicester Chronicle* published a story about a similar notice that had been placed in the *Morning Herald* only a few months previously. Some of the identical phrases were used:

> willing to confide her future happiness to one in every way qualified to render the marriage state desirable …
> Many very happy marriages have taken place through means similar to this now resorted to

The gentleman who had placed the advertisement was mocked: 'how modest! … How winning! … How disinterested! … how knowing!' The story ended with the prophetic warning:

We never heard of more than one marriage that was produced by means of this description, and in that instance the advertiser, as it may be well supposed, was an impostor, who deceived his unfortunate dupe, and most likely himself too, for the marriage was altogether an unhappy one.[1]

William Corder must have seen the earlier advertisement – and would not have seen the piece in the *Leicester Chronicle*.[*] He decided that he liked some of the phrasing; perhaps he visited the offices of the *Morning Herald* and perused some back numbers looking for inspiration. It seems likely that the approximately *one hundred* women who responded to his two advertisements had likewise not seen the earlier story.

A few days after Corder's first advertisement was published, he had a nasty shock. On 19 November, he chanced to meet Peter Mathews in the street near Somerset House in London, close to where Mathews had his London apartment in Clement's Inn. Mathews asked him if he had forwarded the letter he had given him to Maria, because he was very surprised not to have heard from her. He asked where Maria was, and was told that she was in the Isle of Wight. He said that Thomas Martin had written to him and that the Martins were 'uneasy' regarding Maria's whereabouts. He asked whether Corder had married her yet and was told that he had not yet 'settled his affairs'.

According to Foster the stationer, Corder received 'above forty letters' responding to the insertion in the *Morning Herald*, and these he collected. He did not bother to collect the letters resulting from his *Sunday Times* advertisement, another fifty-three, and when Foster became aware of Corder's trial for murder, he realized that he had been given an opportunity to make some money. He published the letters

---

[*] The story had been reprinted from *The Examiner*, 'A Sunday Paper on Politics, Domestic Economy and Theatricals'.

forthwith, omitting names and addresses.[2] Corder did not pick up the second lot of letters because he had apparently found what he was looking for, as he described to Foster, '[a woman] possessed of every quality he could wish.'[3] Two days after the second advertisement was placed, on 27 November 1827 at St Andrew Holborn, he married Mary Moore, spinster, by licence; William was 23, Mary was 31. He said later that he married her about a week after they first met.[4]

Curtis stated that Mary Moore was the lady that Corder met in the Isle of Wight, even though the details in the letter to George Gardiner, which Curtis published, make it clear that that was not the case; both women had a brother, but Mary Moore's brother was a jeweller whereas the other lady's brother was a soldier in barracks. Mary Moore was a spinster; the other lady was a widow with a child. Curtis also claimed that Corder and the lady from the Isle of Wight subsequently met entirely by accident in London, and that later, again entirely coincidentally, she responded to his advertisement for a wife. Curtis's version of events was obviously wrong. On 24 April, there were full accounts of the affair in the newspapers, gleaned from the 'Lambeth Street Correspondent'. It was said, from information from Mary's brother, that Corder met Mary Moore:

> Through the medium of a matrimonial advertisement at
> a pastry-cook shop in Fleet Street.*

He also said that his sister had known Corder for only nine weeks before they were married. She must have told him this story, ashamed to tell her mother and brother that she had known Corder for barely seven days before the wedding.

Mary Moore kept a boarding school at Gray's Inn Terrace and her brother, Charles, had his jeweller's workshop on

---

* This was before Foster had published the replies to Corder's advertisement
so only Foster, Corder, and Mary Moore knew the truth about it.

the same premises. She had spent some time in France as governess to a family, and had purchased the lease on Gray's Inn Terrace on her return. She had some 'small personal property' and income from investments, the result of a legacy from her father. It was reported that she was 'frequently troubled with deafness'. According to Curtis, Mary's brother only found out about his sister's intended nuptials when he came home and found the table set for three. However, the newlyweds had decided to move. Corder's motivation for this might have been his unexpected meeting with Peter Mathews; his London apartments in Clement's Inn were not much more than half a mile away from Gray's Inn Terrace and too close for comfort. If Mathews encountered Corder with his new wife, or found out about her, he would demand answers and the deception would be revealed. Corder may have persuaded Mary to move because being from the country he told her that he could not abide living in the city. Since the Corders were going to leave, the lease on the house would need to be disposed of and an advertisement was placed in *The Times*:

> GRAY'S-INN-TERRACE. – To be LET, for a term of years, an excellent HOUSE, consisting of 12 rooms, with a workshop in the garden fitted up for a Goldsmith. Part of the house is let to respectable lodgers. Particulars may be known by applying to William Corder, Esq., 6, Gray's-inn-terrace.[5]

The advertisement was published on 3 December 1827, six days after Corder had married Mary Moore. Curtis said that Charles Moore only discovered by accident that his place of work was put up for sale by his new brother-in-law, and 'prevented the clandestine negociation [sic]'. It seems difficult to believe that even Foxy Corder would have done this without consulting Charles first. Nevertheless, one thing is very odd: Corder was keen to keep his whereabouts secret from Peter Mathews, not to mention the Martins, yet he broadcast his name and address in London in the most widely read daily newspaper.

The Corders had decided to advertise offering to pay £100 for an established ladies' boarding school 'near town'. A Mrs Ingleton ran such an establishment at Grove House*, Ealing Lane, Brentford and responded to the Corders' advertisement. The *Ipswich Journal* reported:

> this advertisement caught the attention of a lady named Ingleton, who, with her two daughters, had a respectable seminary ... at Ealing ... and as Mrs Ingleton was about to quit her establishment, and wished her daughters to remain, she answered the advertisement , and entered into a treaty with Mr and Mrs Corder[6]

Grove House was on the southern border of Ealing, and was, until the establishment in 1828 of the parish of Old Brentford, within the parish of Ealing. Ealing, less than six miles from Hyde Park, benefited from a healthy environment. The prevailing wind came from the west, so the smoke and unpleasant vapours of London were blown in the opposite direction. It was an area mainly given over to market gardening and schools, and was a positive 'Education Industry' at the time. There were schools for boys and schools for girls. Lady Byron's Ealing Grove Industrial School for Boys opened shortly after the Corders arrived, and Great Ealing School was just up the road by St Mary's Church; the headmaster there was Dr Nicholas, and Thomas Huxley and John Henry Newman would be alumni. Huxley was born in Ealing and would have been three years old when the Corders moved there.

It should have been a delightful environment for William Corder, semi-rural and surrounded by young ladies; his new wife was attracted to the area since she had grown up there.[7]

---

* Grove House was on the east side of what is now Ealing Road, just north of the crossing with the Great West Road and M4 motorway.

The newspaper report said that the Corders would become equal partners 'with the daughters' in exchange for 100 guineas; what was probably meant is that the partnership was between Mrs Ingleton and the Corders, with her daughters staying on as pupils. In addition, Corder gave three bills for half the value of the furniture.[*] But the arrangement did not last long; from the same report:

> [Corder] apparently had something that preyed on his spirits; in the day his habits were retiring and repugnant, and he has occasionally been greatly agitated; his nights were sleepless, and he was frequently heard moaning and talking incoherently in his bed-room.

Mrs Moore, William's new mother-in-law, and Mrs Ingleton, commented:

> [Corder] disturbed and threw into the greatest alarm the entire family and children by his unceasing restlessness, his heavy moaning, and his wild and incomprehensible exclamations in his sleep.

This behaviour alarmed the Misses Ingleton, and they persuaded their mother to remove them from the school and dissolve the partnership with the Corders. She agreed to do so if they would pay for her half share in the furniture. This was done and had been finally settled only days before William Corder's arrest.

But something else happened about this time, so extraordinary, that one wonders if William Corder was quite sane. On Monday 14 April 1828, a gentleman, Mr Cooke, arrived at the White Hart Inn at Manningtree kept by Mr Dale. Manningtree is in Essex, on the border with Suffolk, about half way between Colchester and Ipswich and less than ten miles from Polstead. Mr Cooke told Mr Dale that he had a cheque

---

* In this context a bill is a promissory note for future payment

that he wished to get cashed at the bank, Alexander and Co., opposite the hotel. When the bank opened, the gentleman went over and presented a cheque for ninety-three pounds drawn on the Hadleigh branch of the same bank by R Atkins, in favour of himself, Mr Cooke. He asked for cash. Mr Taylor, the chief clerk, said that since he was neither acquainted with Mr Atkins nor indeed with the gentleman, Mr Cooke, it was 'not a usual thing' to cash a cheque for persons unknown to him. Mr Cooke replied that he was well known in the area; he was a farmer at Wenham Hall, and he had received the cheque the previous Saturday from Mr Atkins, a butcher residing at Stratford, as payment for five head of cattle. Mr Taylor replied that he had never seen 'Atkins' on a Hadleigh cheque before. Mr Cooke then asked Mr Dale from the White Hart to come over and vouch for him, which he did, saying that he had 'seen him frequently at his house'.

The cheque was duly cashed, and Mr Cooke left with the money in local five pound and one pound notes. Shortly afterwards, these were exchanged for sovereigns in Ipswich. The cheque, filled out on the pre-printed Hadleigh bank form, was sent to that branch the same evening, when it was discovered that it was a forgery. Mr Atkin*son*, residing at Stratford, denied all knowledge of it. As became apparent a few weeks later, Mr Cooke turned out to be none other than William Corder. His mother banked at the Hadleigh branch of Alexander and Co., and that was probably where the printed cheque form had come from.[8]

Forgery was a capital offence at the time and although most of those convicted were reprieved and sentenced to transportation, there were still occasional executions. What on earth was William Corder doing? Was he really so desperate for money that he would risk his life? Was the money needed to pay off the Ingletons and secure Grove House, or was it something else? Mary Corder said later that she could not understand it because she had the money needed to pay Mrs

Ingleton in the bank. McCormick claimed that Corder was being blackmailed, but since that intelligence emanated from a fictional association with Thomas Griffiths Wainewright*, the idea must be highly questionable.[9] Nevertheless, ninety-three pounds was a substantial amount of money, and Corder must have wanted it quite badly for something.

The true explanation may have been quite straightforward. William Corder had been used to stealing money to finance his lifestyle; he had pilfered money from his father on numerous occasions, and as became clear from an interview with his mother while in prison, he had taken substantial funds from the farm with him when he left Polstead. He had had to finance his living costs since September 1827, and these included paying for a trip around southern England from the Isle of Wight to Plymouth and living in inns for two months, together with the costs of his marriage and the move to Ealing. He was also 'fashionably' dressed; an 'extensive wardrobe, and linen' belonging to him were found at the house in Ealing. He was unlikely to get any more money from the farm in the short term and he had apparently told his new wife that he had an annual income of £400. The reason for marrying Mary Moore was to benefit from her financial resources; either they were not sufficient for his needs or he needed to preserve the fiction that he really did have a substantial income†. It seems likely that he simply ran out of funds and had to replenish his purse.

In the event, it made no difference, because Maria's stepmother had been having dreams about her; a few days after the incident in Manningtree, Ann Martin persuaded her husband Thomas that Maria had been murdered and buried in the Red Barn, and that he should go and look for her there.

---

*  See appendix 4 for an explanation of who Wainewright was and his alleged involvement.

†  Corder's solicitors, as reported by Curtis, commented: 'a greater part of [Mary Corder's] money went in the purchase of the lease, fixtures and furniture of the school [at Ealing]'.

# A Discovery, an Inquest
# and an Arrest

On Saturday 19 April 1828, Thomas Martin decided to search the Red Barn. The Martins had had no word of Maria for six months, and had neither seen nor heard from her since 18 May the previous year. William Corder had fed them excuses regarding why Maria could not write to them: she was too busy or had a bad hand. Then he claimed that she had written to them but the letter was lost, after which he ceased to communicate at all. The circumstances were undoubtedly suspicious: there was the fact that the Martins' little boy, George, had seen Corder with a pickaxe near the barn at a time when he had insisted that he and Maria were on their way to Ipswich. Ann Martin had seen Corder with Maria's umbrella at his brother's funeral; at first he tried to pretend that it belonged to someone else, finally admitting that Maria had lent it to him. There was the fact that Maria had apparently abandoned her beautiful little boy, Thomas Henry, and her 'bad hand' appeared to afflict her for months and months. The so-called 'lost letter' from Maria must have been very upsetting, and when the Martins continued to hear nothing from her, and letters from Corder stopped too, their suspicions must have been aroused.

Ann Martin said that before Christmas 1827 she started having dreams that Maria had been murdered and buried in the Red Barn. She said nothing to Thomas at the time because she did not want him to think her superstitious. But time went on and there was still no news from Maria. Finally Ann did say something, and on that fateful Saturday Thomas Martin took his mole-spike and went to the barn to investigate. William Pryke, the Corders' bailiff and now farm manager, was with him and he afforded Thomas entry to the barn which was usually kept locked. Pryke raked the straw and Thomas probed the ground with his mole-spike. After a 'good while' of 'raking and poking' they found an area of loose stones where the ground appeared to have been disturbed. Thomas thrust in his spike and it came up with something adhering to it that 'smelt … disagreeable'. They removed the earth and found something 'suspicious'. Pryke said they ought to get someone; a Mr Bowtell eventually came and they proceeded to uncover what was clearly a body. Thomas Martin had found his daughter.

The inquest was held the next day, Sunday 20 April 1828, presided over by the coroner for the Liberty of Bury St Edmunds, Mr John Wayman, who was a solicitor in Bury. The body was removed from the hole in the floor of the barn and placed on a door. It was then taken into the light to allow the surgeon, Mr Lawton, to make an examination and the Martin family and the jury to view the remains. The formal coroner's court was then convened at the Cock Inn in Polstead and witnesses were examined. The record of exactly what went on at the inquest is confused. At the first hearing, on 20 April, there were no reporters present and the only reliable record of what was said is in the Prosecution Brief. In the section marked 'Proofs' it states: 'It has been thought best to copy the evidence exactly as given before the coroner.' Each deposition is dated, but these dates vary between 20 April and 3 June 1828, and evidence from individual witnesses taken at different times is grouped together. It is thus impossible to determine the order in which witnesses were examined. The formal verdict of the jury, and committal of William Corder, was made on 25 April although the examinations continued, since the coroner, Mr Wayman, also became the prosecutor in the case. He subsequently instructed counsel for the formal trial of William

Corder in the assize court. It was certainly odd for the judge in one tribunal to become the prosecutor in the subsequent case, and this was commented on by defence counsel and Corder himself during the assize hearing. To further confuse matters in the record of the inquest, the coroner refused to allow any of the newspaper reporters present during the second session, on 25 April, to take notes. Since Curtis was not present during the first session on 20 April, and was almost certainly not there for the subsequent hearing, it is necessary to rely on the Prosecution Brief for a reliable account of what was said.*

Four witnesses were examined on 20 April: Thomas and Ann Martin, Ann Martin junior (Maria's sister) and George Gardiner. Thomas related how his daughter, whom he was sure was the deceased, had gone away with William Corder the previous May, how he said they would get married but it was delayed and how Corder made excuses as to why Maria did not write. He produced the two letters that Corder had sent him from Leadenhall Street. He then said:

> in consequence of my wife informing me that Corder should have brought some things back from the barn I determined to search the barn, which I did yesterday in company with William Pryke

He said nothing about his wife's dreams. He described how they found the body in a hole about a one and a half feet deep, doubled up and lying on its right side. He said: 'I have no doubt in my mind that it is the body of my daughter.' Finally he related the circumstances of William and Maria coming home from Sudbury with the baby, how the baby died, and how it was taken away at night ostensibly to be buried at Sudbury.

---

\* In the introduction to his book, Curtis said that he left London on St Swithin's Day, 15 July, and was in Polstead at the time of the Cherry Fair, 16 and 17 July. From his description of Polstead, it is clear that it was his first visit.

Ann Martin was now examined. She described in detail the clothes Maria was wearing when she left. She identified the earrings and comb taken from the body as Maria's. She added that William Corder had a gun with him, and he had told her it was loaded. She described how Maria had left dressed in men's clothes, following the story Corder had told them about her being 'taken up' for her bastard children, and the rendezvous in the barn. She repeated the excuses Corder had made why Maria did not write. Then she told the inquest that her son George had seen Corder with a pickaxe later in the afternoon when he should have been driving Maria to Ipswich. When she had challenged Corder on this later, he had said it was not him but Tom Akers. Then the crucial evidence:

> Before Christmas I dreamed the deceased was buried in the bay of the barn and I had the same dream afterwards and told my husband of it sometime afterwards.

Thomas Martin said that he wanted to search the barn for any of Maria's things that might have been left there, but Ann had come right out with the real reason. Maria's sister, Ann, was examined next. She confirmed that the body was that of Maria; there was a missing tooth 'from the upper jaw on the left side where my sister had lost one', and the handkerchiefs, shoes, the Leghorn hat, earrings and comb found on the body she knew to be Maria's and she recognized Maria's hair. She also confirmed what her father and stepmother had told the inquest in respect of Maria's leaving, as well as Corder's account of where Maria was staying and the fact that he had a loaded gun with him when they left. Corder's friend, George Gardiner, was examined and produced some letters that William Corder had written to him. He said that he had asked Corder the previous summer 'what he had done' with Maria Martin. Corder had responded, 'I suppose she is all right enough. I believe she is under Mr Mathews' protection at this time.'

It was clear from the evidence given that the body found in the Red Barn was that of Maria Martin. No-one had seen or heard from her since she had gone off with William Corder almost a year previously, and he had acted suspiciously regarding her failure to write to her parents. In addition to that, George Gardiner's evidence made it clear that Corder had been telling different stories to different people regarding Maria's status and whereabouts. The Coroner decided that there was sufficient evidence to justify apprehending William Corder, and Mr Ayres, 'an active constable living in Boxford' was tasked with tracking him down. Ayres was a good choice, because George Gardiner was his brother-in-law, and Gardiner was an 'intimate friend' of William Corder. It was from Gardiner that Ayres learned Corder's last known address, 6 Gray's Inn Terrace in London.

Meanwhile, a grave had been dug in the churchyard, and shortly after the inquest adjourned at six o'clock in the evening, Maria Martin's remains were screwed down into a 'decent coffin', and carried to the church by six men, followed by her father, stepmother, sister and other friends and relations. There were hundreds of people present at the committal which was conducted by the rector of Polstead, Mr John Whitmore. It was not to be Maria's final journey, but more of that later.

The constable, Mr Ayres, travelled to London and went to the Police Office at Lambeth Street. This was the year before Robert Peel had set up the Metropolitan Police; Lambeth Street was in Whitechapel, East London, one of the seven 'police offices' established by the 1792 Middlesex Justices Act.[1] Ayres told the magistrates the reason for his journey, and they despatched '[James] Lea, an active and intelligent officer' to assist him; surprisingly a warrant was not issued, in addition to which, neither man was armed. James Lea, who was 40 years old, was an experienced officer who frequently appeared at the Old Bailey giving evidence against apprehended felons.

Curtis described what happened next, as told to him by Lea. On Monday 21 April, Ayres and Lea called at Gray's Inn Terrace to be told by a servant girl there that the Corders had left around four months previously and had gone to 'reside at a boarding-school somewhere near Brentford'. They went to Brentford, Ayres staying at the Red Lion, while James Lea asked around for anyone with knowledge of the whereabouts of William Corder. Lea did this on his own since Ayres was known to Corder, and they did not want to startle him. After getting nowhere, Lea chanced to ask an old barrowman who remembered 'a load of goods' about four months previously, evidence of removal, at the door of the school kept by 'Miss' Ingleton. Lea returned to the Red Lion, and having confided their mission to the landlord, was introduced by him to a gentleman whose daughter attended the school. Asked whether she had seen a short gentleman wearing spectacles at the school the daughter answered in the affirmative, adding that she had heard him addressed as 'Mr Corder'.

They devised a subterfuge: the father, accompanied by James Lea, would go with his daughter to the school the next morning on a pretext. It seems odd that a responsible police officer would attempt to arrest a suspected murderer who was known to have been armed without being armed himself, without a warrant and involve a member of the public and his daughter to boot. Nevertheless, that is what happened. They came to the school around ten o'clock in the morning. According to one newspaper report, Corder was at breakfast in the parlour in his dressing-gown, in the company of four ladies, timing the boiling of some eggs.[2] He came into the hall and the pupil's father said 'Good morning Mr Corder'; Corder responded, and Lea knew he had his man. It was Tuesday 22 April 1828, nearly eleven months since Maria had disappeared.

Lea advised Corder that in order not to alarm the rest of the household, he could say he was being arrested for debt; he was allowed to finish his breakfast. On being questioned,

Corder denied three times that he knew anyone of the name of Maria Martin. He was searched, and Lea told him that he was to be taken to the Red Lion at Brentford. At this point Charles Moore, Corder's brother-in-law, insisted on knowing the nature of the charge, and expressed astonishment on being told it was murder, commenting on Corder's 'kind, tender-hearted and indulgent' attitude towards his sister. Corder was taken to the Red Lion and left handcuffed to Ayres while Lea returned to search Corder's room at Grove House. He observed a sword which he did not recover at the time but returned for later, and a pair of pistols in a black bag which he took with him. There was a copy of *Fanny Hill* in a trunk, and he found a letter from Corder's sister, probably his unmarried sister Elizabeth, who was under no illusions about William's character:

> William, you know what a horrid liar you are, and you are now in London, a place where there are many temptations – pray avoid them, and leave off your evil ways, and endeavour to become a useful member of society.[3]

Corder dined at the Red Lion accompanied by Lea, Ayres and Charles Moore, after which he was taken to the Lambeth Street Police Station where Matthew Wyatt, the sitting magistrate, just before the office closed, ordered him to be taken to Polstead. Although Curtis does not say so, Corder must have spent the night in the cells. The next morning, Wednesday 23 April, they took the Defiance coach from the Bull at Aldgate to Colchester. This was St George's Day, the day the story broke in the newspapers, probably from a reporter at Lambeth Street; indeed the story in the *Morning Chronicle* the next day was accompanied by a detailed account from their 'Lambeth-street correspondent.' The coach arrived at Colchester at nine o'clock in the evening. According to Curtis, Corder earned further opprobrium by joining in with some obscene conversation on the roof of the coach which 'disgusted [some of] the passengers' when they were acquainted with the 'dreadful charge he had to meet'.

When they arrived at the George Inn, they were greeted by a crowd of people all eager to see Corder. Lea tried to get Corder into Colchester Castle Gaol for the night as he was worried about his security, but Mr Smith, the governor, refused to admit him without a warrant. Lea then resorted to a magistrate, Mr Abel, to persuade the governor to relent but he was adamant. Corder spent the night at the George sharing a bed with Ayres to whom he was handcuffed, the other hand being handcuffed to the bed. He was able, however, to write to his mother:

> Dear Mother – I scarcely dare presume to address you, having a full knowledge of all the shame, disgrace ... for ever a stain on my family

And as if knowing that her one remaining son was accused of murder was not bad enough for Mrs Corder senior, William asked his mother to

> receive Mr Moore on Friday morning, with whom may probably be my injured, lawful, and I must do her the justice to say, worthy and affectionate wife.

From the tenor of the letter it seems likely that this was the first knowledge William's mother had of Mrs Corder junior. The next morning, Thursday 24 April, Corder received a large number of visitors at the inn including Sir William Rowley[4], several magistrates and 'other gentlemen ... of the town'. He was also visited by a clergyman, the Revd Mr Seaman who was apparently acquainted with the Corders. He presented him with a hymnbook, adding, helpfully, that if he were

> guilty of the foul crime imputed to him, he might hope for pardon at a higher tribunal than that before which he would ... shortly ... appear.

Then Corder had to endure the justifiable indignation of his brother-in-law, who was demanding to know how he could send letters saying he was living happily with Maria Martin when he was married to his sister. James Lea, perhaps sensing an impending physical altercation, stepped in pointing out to Mr Moore that such questions were not appropriate 'at the present stage of the business'. Corder seems to have been exhibited like a circus attraction all day at Colchester. Curtis, nevertheless, commented that James Lea's conduct

> throughout this business [was] very creditable to him, and to the establishment to which he belongs

But it was not over. At nine o'clock in the evening there were more visitors, and these must have substantially increased William's misery. Mr Taylor, chief clerk at Alexander's bank at Manningtree arrived, accompanied by Mr Dale, the proprietor of the White Hart Inn, opposite the bank. Mr Taylor was the victim of the fraud, just ten days previously, when 'Mr Cooke', vouched for by Mr Dale, had obtained ninety-three pounds from the bank using a forged cheque. The butcher, 'Mr Atkins' against whose non-existent account the cheque had been drawn, was said to have resided at Stratford, about five miles from Polstead. Taylor said it was 'something ... in the newspaper description of the prisoner' that had induced him and Mr Dale to make the journey to Colchester. The description of William Corder that had been published, so far, was just that he was 24 years old, of florid complexion and fashionable dress. Perhaps that, together with the relative closeness of Polstead to Stratford made them suspicious. Taylor, addressing Corder, demanded repayment of the money. Corder was 'mute with astonishment, and hung down his head'. According to Curtis, Taylor said to him 'Why don't you look me in the face like a man?' Corder flung himself into a chair and hid his face in his hands, neither admitting nor denying the charge. Taylor was, no doubt, very satisfied that he had run down the man who had defrauded his bank for ninety-three pounds. James Lea recollected that Corder had asked him if he had found eighty sovereigns in the drawer of his writing desk when the room had been searched. He had not found any money, and Corder opined that his wife must have removed it.

The departure to Polstead was delayed until midnight at the suggestion of Sir William Rowley and also to avoid the crowds. Rowley had pointed out that by doing so it would be very late when they passed the prisoner's mother's house, and this would afford her the minimum of pain. They arrived in the early hours at the Cock Inn at Polstead and the inquest was reconvened the same day, Friday 25 April, with Corder in an upper room. But now the inquest too was turning into a circus. A long account of the circumstances surrounding the discovery of the murder and the apprehension of William Corder had been published in the newspapers the previous day and Curtis said that between twelve and fifteen reporters were present along with many members of the public. In the first of what might be regarded as 'unconventional actions' on his part, Mr Wayman, the coroner, decided that the press corps could only be permitted to stay provided they took no notes. He cited two precedents: one where it had been pronounced an offence to publish the results of an inquest before the accused had been tried, and a case where the coroner had been censured by the judge for allowing it to be done. Two representatives of the press argued against this ruling but to no avail. For the order of witnesses examined, Curtis's account is followed; for the content of their evidence – since the press were not allowed to take notes – the Prosecution Brief is used.

The first witness was John Baalham, constable of Polstead. He declared that he had never had a warrant for the apprehension of Maria Martin for giving birth to bastard children. At this point, Mr Humphreys, a London solicitor engaged to represent William Corder, asked the coroner to allow his client to be present to hear the charges laid against him. It should not have been an unreasonable request; the coroner had ordered constable Ayres to bring Corder to Polstead, and he was now secured in an upstairs room. The coroner, appearing to decline the request, Humphreys cited a couple of precedents where this was allowed. Mr Wayman nevertheless ruled that Corder could not be present during the hearing of witnesses, although he would have the depositions read to him.

The next witness was George Martin, Maria's ten-year-old half-brother. He was noted as a 'little and very intelligent boy'. He confirmed that 'not long before evening' on the day that Maria had left, while he was collecting grass for his donkey, he had seen Corder leave the Red Barn with a pickaxe on his shoulder and go in the direction of his house. He confirmed that Corder had a loaded gun and that Maria was crying when she had left the Martins' cottage.

Phoebe and Francis Stow were examined next. They lived in the cottage closest to the Red Barn. Sometime the previous May, just after one o'clock, William Corder had asked Phoebe Stow if he could borrow one of her husband's spades. She was not sure of the date, but it was between 29 April, when she was 'confined' and 29 May, and he could not stop to talk because he was in a hurry; he was wearing a velveteen coat. Her husband's contribution was that William Corder was the master of Mrs Corder's farm; the first corn that was harvested was taken into the bay in the Red Barn where Maria's body had been discovered, and Corder had been present either for the first or the second load of corn that was brought in. He did say that Corder had offered him a pound note if he would cut his (Corder's) throat, although he was smiling when he said it.

James Lea was examined, and related how he had arrested Corder at Grove House. On searching Corder's room he found a passport for France, dated 20 December 1827, some letters and

65

a black velvet reticule [bag] … containing the pair of
pistols … name Harcourt, Ipswich, a flask with balls and
powder therein [and] a mould for balls

Lea added that Corder told him that he had purchased the
pistols when he was 10 years old. The coroner commented
that 'the detonating principle [using percussion caps] was a
much more recent invention'. Percussion caps were introduced
around 1820. Previously, firearms had a small pan of primer
gunpowder which was ignited by a flint striking steel; this
set off the main charge in the gun, but was prone to misfire in
damp weather. The percussion cap was much more reliable,
since a hammer striking the cap would detonate a small charge
of mercury fulminate or something similar, and this would
ignite the main charge. Corder's pistols used percussion caps,
and since these had only been introduced around eight years
previously, his guns must have been purchased more recently
than when he was ten years old.

Ann Martin, Maria's stepmother was now re-examined,
and burst into tears on being shown the black reticule bag
saying that it had belonged to Maria. She related the arguments
between Maria and William Corder over the five-pound note
that he had taken; Maria had accused him of taking bread out
of their mouths, and more than once she had heard Maria say,
in respect of the note, that if she went to prison, so should he.
She detailed the clothes that Maria was wearing when she
left, adding that Maria also had a green umbrella and William
Corder was wearing a velveteen coat.

The next witness was William Towns who had laboured
on the Corders' farm for seventeen years. He heard William
Corder give the order to fill with wheat the bay where Maria
Martin's body had been found. Before that, the bay had been
littered with straw so the actual gravel and earth floor could
not be seen. Ann Martin was recalled and shown the various

items recovered from Maria Martin's body; she identified all except a coat as having belonged to Maria.

Robert Offord, a cutler at Hadleigh, confirmed that Corder had, the previous year, brought in a small sword he wanted sharpened 'as sharp as a carving knife'. It had a scimitar (curved) blade, and a brass-mounted white handle; it was twelve to thirteen inches long. Corder told him that he was required to sit at the head of a table at his cousin's wedding, and wanted to carve with it.

Lastly, the surgeon, John Lawton, who had examined Maria's body was called to give evidence. Since his evidence was critical, it is reproduced mostly verbatim with some adjustment to the punctuation:

[The body] had not been disturbed when I saw it but merely the earth removed from the upper part. The body was removed from the ground and placed on the barn door in the light. It was much decomposed from having lain a long time in the ground. I examined it as carefully as I possibly could and I assisted in taking off the clothes. The first thing I took hold of was a piece of sack. I pulled it off the face and I pulled other parts of the sack from various parts of the body. I found the body lying on the right side with the head forced down upon the right shoulder. There was an appearance upon the face which convinced me that there had been blood there, and I found blood upon the clothes, and upon the green striped handkerchief which was tied very tight round the neck. The handkerchief had apparently been pulled tight about the neck and there was a space between the outer fold of it and the tight part sufficient for a hand to have been inserted. In the neck just below the fold of the handkerchief there was the appearance of a wound inflicted by some sharp instrument but the part was in such a state of decomposition that I can only state it had that appearance. There also appeared to have been injury inflicted in the orbit of the right eye, it appeared as if something had been thrust in, and had occasioned fracture of the internal bones of the orbit and nose. There did not appear to be any gown over the body. There were a flannel petticoat or shift, stays, stockings and high shoes; the several things found on the body were delivered to John Baalham the constable. I took the green handkerchief off the neck myself. I then proceeded to examine the internal parts of the head, but the brain was in a fluid state from the length of time it had been buried so that I cannot state what injury it had received. The left orbit of the eye was sound. The bone which divides the nose into the two nostrils was displaced and on the right side the bones were materially injured apparently a pointed instrument thrust into the eye causing fracture of the bones of the nose and orbit. I pointed these things to the jury as I found them. I examined the chest and abdomen and found no injury anywhere within the body. I found two small portions of bone in the throat. Supposing an injury to have been received in the bones of the nose and orbit these pieces might have got into the throat through the mouth or they might have fallen down from decay. The left hand was separated from the wrist and was lying on the body. This might have arisen from decay. The other handkerchief and the shift had blood upon them, considerable appearances of blood. I am of the opinion the deceased's death proceeded from violence. A jab in the eye with a knife or a sharp instrument would certainly have caused the injury which I found but it was impossible to discover whether there was injury done to the fleshy parts of the eye or face from the state of decomposition in which they were. A sharp instrument introduced as I have mentioned might have penetrated the brain

... a mortal injury might have been caused by a sharp instrument penetrated in the parts I found fractured. I am of the opinion that the green handkerchief was so tightly pulled round the neck that strangulation might have been caused thereby. I removed the handkerchief principally myself and minutely examined its removal and I am satisfied that it could not have been so tied round in a natural way. The neck appeared compressed from the tightness of the handkerchief. The sack had been tied up and I had the string with which the mouth of the sack was tied in my hand.

In view of subsequent events, Mr Lawton's evidence is most important. He had examined the body as it had been removed from the ground and found clear indications of unnatural death in the wounds to the face and neck, the blood on the handkerchief and shift and the tightness of the handkerchief about the throat.

The coroner then indicated that all the witnesses had been examined, and Mr Humphreys asked that his client be allowed to come and hear the evidence against him read through. James Lea brought in the handcuffed prisoner who was dressed in a large Spanish cloak. The evidence taken on Sunday was read through to him, but he seemed inattentive and unable to concentrate. Mr Humphreys then suggested that perhaps it would be best if Corder were to retire and he would read the evidence through to him privately. Before he left, the coroner told him he was charged with the wilful murder of Maria Martin, and asked him if he had anything to say. After talking to his attorney, he declined to say anything and left the room with James Lea.

Wayman addressed the jury; he told them that there was no doubt that a murder had been committed and it was their job to decide whether there was sufficient evidence pointing towards William Corder as the murderer. He offered to summarize the evidence but this was deemed unnecessary. The jury retired for half an hour, and on their return, the foreman declared a unanimous verdict of wilful murder against William Corder. The coroner then issued a warrant against the governor of Bury Gaol, Mr Orridge, to take the prisoner into his custody until the next assizes.

Curtis noted that during these solemn proceedings, a large party was going on elsewhere in the Cock Inn, with singing of 'objectionable songs' and 'other symptoms of boisterous mirth' that the landlord, Michael Gordon, was entirely unable to control.

# Problems with the Prosecution, not to mention the Defence

John Wayman, the coroner who had presided over the inquest into the death of Maria Martin, now instituted a prosecution against William Corder. Whether or not this was unusual at the time is unclear, but he proceeded to instruct counsel, and a prosecution case against William Corder for the murder of Maria Martin was prepared. But it is evident that there were problems. The circumstantial evidence against Corder was overwhelming; the newspapers were full of it, and they were sure that Corder was the murderer. But circumstantial evidence cannot, and should not, be sufficient to convict in a capital case. Maria Martin had been murdered, and a substantial part of the prosecution case, wasted effort as it turned out, was devoted to proving that the body found in the Red Barn was hers. The inquest revealed that she may have died from a 'jab in the eye', a possible penetrative wound to the throat and/or strangulation with a handkerchief. Where was the direct evidence to link her death to the prisoner? Wayman may well have instructed counsel, and they probably told him that he had a very poor case against William Corder.

A chance remark may have saved the day. Curtis reported – although his dates were wrong – that Mr Chaplin, probably Henry Robert Chaplin a surgeon from Lavenham, and a 'Mr Glover', provenance unknown, were discussing the case. Glover was obviously involved in some capacity because he had access to the evidence. He was not one of the inquest jury; he may have been one of Mr Wayman's staff. Later on, another surgeon, John Charles Nairn, was probably referring to Glover when he described him as a 'scientific gentleman present at the inquest'. Chaplin was saying that Mr Lawton, the surgeon present when Maria's body was first examined on 20 April, was now of the view that the wound to the head was caused by a pistol ball that had

> entered the neck of the deceased about the jugular, and that it took an oblique direction to the eye on the opposite side of the head

Glover observed that whether Maria had been shot or not, she had certainly been stabbed in the side, because he had examined the stays and 'chemise' and found a wide cut made with a 'broad sharp instrument, which had evidently been stabbed into her body'. Chaplin examined the clothes and confirmed to his own satisfaction that there was such a cut. This information was then passed to Mr Wayman in his capacity as coroner/prosecutor. Should they exhume the body to check whether Maria had been stabbed in the side? According to Curtis, there was a difference of opinion, but the majority took the view that it should be done. Present at the event, which in true Gothic style took place between three and four o'clock in the morning on Monday 19 May, by lantern light, were John Baalham, the parish clerk/constable, Mr John Charles Nairn, a surgeon from Dedham, Mr Henry Chaplin, the surgeon from Lavenham, and the men doing the digging. Mr Lawton was unable to attend but sent his assistant, Mr Bewick in his place. Nairn found the stab wound in the left side of the body corresponding to the cut in the shift, and removed the heart and the two ribs through which the knife thrust had been made for further analysis. The original conversation that led to the exhumation turned upon Lawton's view that a pistol shot had made the head wound. He had formed that opinion from studying the skull. Maria's head was removed at some point and was produced during the trial in August. Lawton must have removed it for study during his initial examination of the body on 20 April, and this was confirmed during his subsequent evidence during the trial. What was left of Maria was reburied before the curious were abroad since there were no immediate reports of the exhumation in the newspapers.

The Prosecution Brief contains a number of statements sworn on 3 June 1828, together with one dated 27 May and some undated. There is no indication that Mr Wayman took the statements, although comments made by defence counsel during the subsequent trial suggest that he did. On 27 May, Phoebe Stow related a conversation she had with William Corder the previous summer around harvest time. She had asked him about the child Maria had had at Sudbury; he told her it was dead and buried and that Maria would 'have no more'. The conversation, which is reproduced in full in the chapter on the trial, was to the effect that Maria would have no more children, Corder was damned if she would, and she was close by where he could go to her any time she liked. The conversation had taken place in Phoebe Stow's house, which was the closest dwelling to the Red Barn.

It was on 3 June that most of the rest of the depositions were sworn. Rachael Bugg's status was not clear, but from the context she seems to have been a servant working for the Corders. Her husband was a long-time labourer for them. Corder, she said, 'came to the farmhouse in which I live' and asked if she had heard the news, since 'everyone' was saying that he was to take Maria home to be Rachael Bugg's mistress. Corder told her that Maria would never be her mistress, that she had gone to France in a steam packet where he hoped she would be safe.

Mrs Ann Martin made two further statements. She listed the items that Maria had taken with her when she left; she also detailed the events which led up to Maria's departure, reiterating that Corder had a brace of pistols. She related how she saw Maria's umbrella, which she had taken with her when she left, in Corder's possession and how he had changed his story regarding how he came to have it.

John Charles Nairn, the surgeon from Dedham, related what happened during the exhumation. He commented on the good state of preservation of the chest and abdomen cavities such that any 'penetrating' injury into either could be easily detected. There was a cut in the right ventricle of the heart which Mr Lawton had made during his initial examination on 20 April. Examining the interior surface of the ribs, Nairn described a 'one inch' cut he had found between the fifth and sixth ribs on the left side, and declared that it was of 'long standing'. On further examination of the heart, he found a cut

> about two inches from the apex of the heart ... the direction of this cut corresponds with the wound in the ribs

Furthermore, it corresponded with the cut in the shift. He opined that, from the description he had been given, the 'dirk or instrument' found by Mr Lea at Corder's house could have made the wound. He now commented on the head wound(s):

> I have since inspected the head of the deceased ... I concur with Mr Lawton as to a thrust having been made through the orbit penetrating into the sphenoidal sinus and ... I observed the track of a ball which appears to have entered the left superior maxillary or jawbone just above the second or third grinder teeth passing through the posterior part of the nose and ... making its exit at the right orbit. In my opinion ... it was a ball from a pistol and that the person who fired it must have stood rather behind the deceased ... I should be of the opinion the stab through the orbit was made after the wound thus produced by the pistol ball.

John Lawton now stated his findings on the examination of the head:

I have re-examined the head of Maria Martin and have made a section of the cheek bone on the right side with a view of examining the parts more accurately. Upon thoroughly cleaning the bones I distinctly discovered the track of a ball which I am of opinion had passed into the jawbone above the second or third grinder teeth on the left side of the face through the cheek bone and the posterior parts of the nose making its exit at the right orbit and which accounts for the destruction of the bones of the nose and orbit mentioned in my former deposition and I have no doubt of the first attempt at the deceased's life having been made by a ball fired in that direction – and I am now of the opinion that the stabs mentioned in my former deposition in the orbit and neck were inflicted after the injury above mentioned. I have also seen the heart and know that the wound in the right ventricle mentioned by Mr Nairn was made by myself, but the other wound I am of the opinion was made by a thrust which corresponds with the wound between the ribs and with a hole in the shift. I am now satisfied that the thrust, which in my former deposition I stated might have entered the brain did not, but penetrated into the sphenoidal sinus.

Henry Chaplin, the surgeon from Lavenham, commented that he agreed fully with Mr Nairn's conclusions.

Finally, William Pryke made a statement. He was with Thomas Martin when Maria's body was discovered; surprisingly, he was not called to give evidence at the inquest. It was he who discovered the loose earth in the right-hand bay of the barn; they had tried three other parts of the barn first. He said that great care was taken in removing the earth from the body so as not to disturb it. William Pryke had known Corder from his infancy; the last time he saw him was the 19 September 1827 when he drove him to Colchester for the

London coach. Corder spoke of Maria Martin saying: 'After I am gone there will be various reports respecting her and me.' He 'spoke very highly of her and said he thought she was a well meaning girl'. He also said that he hadn't seen Maria since the previous May. Pryke then made a curious comment:

> I did say to the wife of John Bugg senior that she had better keep a conversation she had with William Corder to herself and it was this woman I alluded to in a conversation I had with Mrs Stow.

There were also several undated depositions listed in the Prosecution Brief; the significant elements of which are listed in the order in which they were given.

William Martin was a cousin of Maria's. He said that he met Corder the previous August saying 'How do you do cousin?' alluding to the fact that Maria and Corder were married. He said that Corder appeared 'slightly offended' at which William Martin observed 'You ought to have known better than to marry a w[hore]'. Corder replied: 'You ought to know better than to call another man's wife a w[hore]...You kicked her bottom once'. William Martin responded 'Perhaps I shall again'. Corder responded 'Aye, but you never will kick her again'. Corder apparently invited Martin into his house for some beer and they continued to talk about Maria, although Corder told him not to talk too loud in case the people in the house would hear. Lastly Martin asked Corder where Maria was; he replied 'she is where I can see her any day when I like'.

Peter Mathews related the story of the 'missing' five-pound note and how he had applied to Sir Francis Freeling, 'Secretary of the Post Office', to investigate. In July 1827 (mistakenly written '1828'), Mathews had 'several interviews with the prisoner'. Corder eventually confessed to having taken the note, and had 'much difficulty in prevailing on [Maria] to write the letter' sent to the Colchester Post Office saying that she had, after all, received the note. Corder was afraid for his life if he were found guilty of stealing the note. Corder told Mathews that Maria was living near Yarmouth*; when he met him in November in London, he was told she was in the Isle of Wight.

Henry Harcourt remembered Corder bringing him a pair of percussion pistols, like those recovered by Lea, on 28 February 1827. He added that percussion pistols were not common and 'did not become general until somewhere about 1820'. William Chaplin deposed that 'Stoke Fair' was on 16 May 1827 and that the Red Barn was clear of corn by that date.† Thomas Akers would prove that he did not go across any of the fields leaving from the Red Barn on 18 May 1827.

That was the sum total of the evidence from which to prepare a prosecution case against William Corder. The circumstantial evidence was even more damning than before, but there seemed to be proof now that as well as possibly having been strangled, Maria had been shot by a pistol and stabbed with a knife, and Corder was found with a pair of pistols and a dirk or small sword. There was still no unequivocal proof that he did it, but the case against him was stronger; the dimensions of the pistol-balls recovered from Corder's house in Ealing were consistent with the damage to Maria's skull. His comments to Phoebe Stow, Rachael Bugg and William Martin though, betray a level of stupidity that is verging on the incomprehensible. It was almost as though he wanted to be found out; nevertheless, it was still all circumstantial evidence.

At this point it is appropriate to leave Mr Wayman struggling with the evidence, trying to weave it into a watertight prosecution case, and see what the defence were up to, because they too were having problems. It is said that wars are lost rather than won, and perhaps the same applies to legal cases. The difficulties that the prosecution were having,

---

* (Great) Yarmouth, Norfolk.

† It was the date of Stoke Fair, on 16 May 1827, that allowed the Martins to be sure of the date, two days later, that Maria had last been seen.

lacking direct evidence, should have played straight into the defence hands and juries can be fickle. On the other hand there had been so much publicity attaching to the case, so much background material published in the newspapers, how was an unbiased jury to be found? How was a case to be made against the overwhelming circumstantial evidence against Corder? How could the principle of 'Beyond Reasonable Doubt' convince a jury not to convict?

The solicitor initially charged with looking after Corder's defence case was Mr Charles Humphreys of Broadway, Ludgate Hill, in London. It should have been a good choice; Humphreys was an experienced solicitor in criminal cases who was probably retained by Mrs Corder junior. However, another solicitor also became interested in the case; he was Mr Richard Charnock of Appleby and Charnock, of Gray's Inn. According to Curtis he was 'long acquainted with Corder's friends'. Elsewhere it was stated that he was related to the Corders. He, apparently, advised that the case should be made that Maria had shot herself following the quarrel, having previously stolen one of Corder's pistols, and Corder's friends all agreed with this approach. Humphreys thought it to be a very dangerous one, calling it 'a most desperate course'. He might have reminded them that the surgeon, John Nairn, had suggested that the person who fired the pistol was standing 'rather behind the deceased', not a viable firing-angle for a suicide, although it seems likely that Nairn's evidence, sworn after the inquest, was not made available to the defence team. Curtis reported that Humphreys initially wished Corder to say nothing in the trial, and let his counsel handle the case. His position was that the only way to save Corder's life was to admit that he shot Maria under extreme provocation during the quarrel, and plead to a lesser crime of manslaughter. That would certainly get him transported, probably for life, but it might save him from the scaffold. Curtis must have been mistaken in the detail of this, because the law at the time prevented a defendant charged with a felony from allowing counsel to address the jury on his behalf. Curtis then said that Humphreys conceded that Corder could defend himself and make his defence statement in court. It is interesting to note that not long after this the Prisoners' Counsel Act, 1836, changed the law such that the defendant did have the right to professional counsel to conduct his or her defence. However, Corder's friends were adamant, he would claim in court that Maria committed suicide; on that basis, even though Humphreys was offered a 'large fee' to conduct the defence, he declined. Curtis says that various barristers were approached to conduct the defence case. Mr Adolphus asked for 200 guineas plus expenses; Sergeant Andrews agreed to 100 guineas, but later withdrew. Finally Mr Brodrick* agreed to do the job for 140 guineas.

Corder meanwhile was languishing in gaol. Naturally there was great interest in the newspapers in the forthcoming trial; *The Observer*, on 3 August 1828, had a lengthy story from its own reporter in Bury St Edmunds. The trial, it said, was the only topic of conversation. Many considered that Corder might be acquitted, on the basis that his indifference to the whole proceeding could only be explained by his innocence. The newspaper reported that Corder had conveyed his 'reversionary property' to his wife's mother for '£200'. Corder's wife, 'far advanced in pregnancy', visited him every morning at eleven o'clock; *The Standard* reported:

> She is much older than he is (about 36 years of age), of a lady-like appearance, and although her countenance is not prepossessing, her figure is good.[1]

Corder also had visits from his mother and sister. His mother, 'a care-worn old lady' was concerned about £400 which he had received for some grain sold before he left home in September

---

* Curtis spelled his name 'Broderick', and that spelling was also used elsewhere. His entry in the *Law Lists* and his obituary in 1830 in the *Legal Observer* use 'Brodrick', and that spelling is adopted here.

the previous year. If the report is to be believed, Corder reproached his mother for not having 'paid that attention to his wife to which she was entitled.' His mother responded that the first time she had seen his wife was when she came to Polstead with a solicitor and

> demanded an inspection of all the family papers, for the purpose of ascertaining what property he was entitled to

Mrs Corder senior could

> scarcely believe they were married, when she reflected upon the extraordinary manner in which they became connected.

The report also described the visit of 'Miss Corder'. This was Elizabeth Corder, William's unmarried older sister. She was dressed 'almost in the extreme of fashion' and drove to the prison in a pony chaise. According to an eyewitness, she 'flounced into the room' saying, 'How do you do, William, I am glad to see you?' The meeting was described as 'heartless', and after a short while, Elizabeth Corder left in her chaise.[2]

It is possible to have some sympathy for William's family, old and new, given the circumstances. He had embezzled a considerable amount of money from the farm during the three months he was in sole charge; his mother was concerned about £400, equivalent to around £20,000 today. She had lost a husband and three sons in the space of less than three years, and her one remaining son was about to go on trial for his life. It is no wonder that she looked careworn. William's sister might have been wondering how *she* was to be kept in the manner to which she was accustomed, given that William had been raiding the family finances and they were dependent on a farm manager to keep things going and provide an income.

William's wife was in a worse predicament. She was six months pregnant and faced with the fact that not only had the man she married in good faith been charged with murder, but he had been telling tales about having married Maria and had passed a forged cheque – a capital offence. Mrs Corder junior had either paid back or was about to pay back the ninety-three pounds William stole from the bank, and she was facing a considerable legal bill for William's defence. She had also lost her living; it was not remotely likely that anyone would send young lady pupils to a school run by the wife of a probable murderer.

In addition to which both mother and wife, loving William in their different ways, must have been worried sick that he really might be found guilty with the inevitable consequence.

# The Trial

The assizes at Bury St Edmunds allowed the town to indulge itself in the greatest of ceremony. The judges arrived on Saturday, 2 August 1828, accompanied by the 'high sheriff, the under-sheriff and a number of javelin-men'.* They proceeded to the Crown Court at the Shire Hall where the King's Commission was read by the clerk of the assizes. Although there seemed to be confusion in some quarters as to exactly when Corder's trial was to take place, it had been fixed for Thursday 7 August. The trial judge was to be the Lord Chief Baron of the Court of the Exchequer, Baron Alexander. The legal career of William Alexander was not exactly a glittering affair. Born in Scotland, and with an estate at Airdrie, he spent more than forty years in the Court of Chancery. He had been Master of Chancery for the last fifteen years of his term there, when in January 1824,

> to the surprise, and somewhat to the dissatisfaction of the profession ... he was raised to the Head of the Court of the Exchequer ... notwithstanding his own doubts and those entertained by the legal world in general, he presided most ably for seven years

In 1831 he was 'induced to resign' to make way for Lord Lydhurst, but he appears to have been not too concerned; iron ore had been found on his Airdrie estate making a 'large accession to his fortune.'[1]

---

\* The Javelin Men were ushers or guards armed with spears 'in the retinue of a sheriff ... who escorted the judges at the assizes.' *OED*

A man was to be tried for his life, but the proceedings outside the court on that rainy Thursday morning descended into chaos. The assize hearings had started on Monday and had been accompanied by 'dense crowds' unsure of when the Corder trial would start. But for the day of Corder's trial, according to Curtis, Baron Alexander had issued a strict instruction that none of the public, under pain of dire consequences, was to be allowed into the court until he had taken his seat. This stricture was repeated in *The Times*.[2] *The Standard* reported that one of the counsel, incensed by the rudeness of the 'javelin-men' enforcing the order, went to speak to the Lord Chief Baron at the Sheriff's house. He, 'with some indignation, disclaimed having given any such order'. *The Standard* report went on:

> [The Lord Chief Baron] had expressed a wish that the people should be let in by degrees. It was especially his wish that counsel should be admitted the moment they presented themselves.[3]

The effect of the ruling, as enforced by the javelin men, was that the crowds were even denser than normal outside the court on that day. Various reports stated that the entrances to the court had been besieged since as early as five o'clock in the morning notwithstanding the wet weather. *The Times* reported that the barristers were attempting to force their way to the door, 'sweating and struggling against ... the crowd'. According to Curtis, two of the counsel had their wigs 'hooked off' and one was 'disgowned'. At around twenty minutes before nine, Mr Orridge, the prison governor, appeared at a window and asked for newspaper reporters and persons there 'for literary purposes' to come forward and present their tickets of entry, but it was impossible to get near the door. Contrary cries went up: 'No preference – a court of justice is free and open to all' was countered by 'Let the gentlemen pass, or, as we shall not get in unless they do, we shall know nothing about it'. Of the counsel, magistrates and jurors attempting to gain entrance, some lost their hats, some their pocket-books, and others their money – and not a few the lappets of their coats.

Some enterprising aspirants, had

[raised ladders] ... and numbers, (ladies among the rest) actually mounted the tiling of a house, from whence they could obtain an indistinct view of the prisoner

Orders had been given to exclude ladies from the court, but those who had been unable to gain entry were unperturbed:

a number of them ... stood at the risk of their lives, on the stone ledges and basements of the windows of the court ... there was a dreadful thunder-storm [which] could not damp the curiosity of those beautiful spectators ... Several of the side windows were broken, from the pressure of the throng

Other people had managed to climb on to the roof of the court building, and 'lying flat on the joists' were able to peer down over a circular skylight into the courtroom. Curtis said they looked like 'bodiless and wingless angels'. Mr Orridge directed them to withdraw or risk the ceiling coming down with dreadful consequences for all. A guard was posted to prevent a recurrence. Curtis noted that despite the exclusion order on 'females', exceptions were made for the wives of the sheriff and chaplain, and 'two others, who found their way to the bench'.[4]

Corder had arrived with Mr Orridge around half-past eight, and was taken to a cell in the court building. The Lord Chief Baron's entrance was delayed for twenty minutes while the javelin men attempted to force a way through for him; *The Times* reported that he was 'carried off his legs' at one point by the crowd. There was some sentencing of prisoners to be done first, and then the jurors for the trial were called. According to the *Morning Chronicle*, there was an hour's delay in finding them; because of the press of the crowd outside, they had to be 'brought over the heads of the crowd'. They arrived some having lost shoes, some coats, 'and nearly fainting'. The correspondent had never witnessed anything like it; the scene, he said, 'beggars all description'.[5]

Finally, William Corder was brought into court at a quarter-past ten. Two of the jury were challenged by Mr Brodrick, and 'after a great deal of delay, a jury was impaneled [sic] and sworn'. The indictment was read by Mr Edgell, the Clerk of the Arraigns. Curtis described the indictment as a 'masterly specimen of legal skill and exactitude' anticipating that it would become a model for the future. Mr Wayman, the coroner/prosecutor and his legal team, must have spent a considerable amount of time constructing it. Stripped of the legal circumlocution, the indictment charged Corder with ten counts (Curtis only counted nine); first, that he shot Maria Martin in the face with a two-shilling pistol; second that he stabbed her between the ribs; third, that he stabbed her in the face; fourth, that he stabbed her in the neck; fifth, that he strangled her with a handkerchief; sixth, that he shot her in the face with a ten-shilling gun; seventh, that he suffocated her by burying her alive; eighth, that he suffocated her by burying her in a hole, two feet deep, two feet wide and six feet long; ninth, that he stabbed and strangled her; tenth, that he shot, stabbed, strangled and suffocated her by burying her alive. This indictment smacked more of desperation than 'skill and exactitude'. The prosecution team had no idea how Maria Martin had actually died; it seems that they decided to permutate all of the various options in the hope that one of the charges would stick. When he had finished reading the indictment, Edgell addressed Corder:

William Corder, are you guilty of the murder of Maria Martin, or not guilty?

Corder replied 'Not guilty, my Lord'. He also pleaded not guilty to the charge of the inquest. A scale model of the Red Barn was placed on a table in the court, and the judge and others were supplied with plans of the surrounding fields. Both defence and prosecution witnesses were obliged to leave the court to be accommodated in an adjoining room. Prosecution attorneys were Mr Andrews and Mr Kelly. It is not clear who was leading, but Mr Andrews conducted the bulk of the examination of witnesses and made the opening statement summarizing the facts of the case as known. Defending was Mr Brodrick; he had Mr Prendergast with him, but the latter made very little contribution.

Comparison of various newspaper accounts of the trial and Curtis's own narrative reveals some oddities. Most of the reports are obviously written by different people, although surgeon Lawton's testimony is word for word identical in *The Times*, the *Sunday Times*, *The Standard* and the *Morning Chronicle*; only Curtis's account differs in the wording. Elsewhere some of the reporting is in error, as in *The Times* and the 'spike' discovered underground[*], as well as Nairn's testimony and the heart divested of its *developing* membrane.[†] It is also quite difficult to believe that the reporter from *The Times* and the one from *The Standard* attended the same proceedings. *The Times*, in respect of Corder's appearance:

> [Corder] appeared to be about 40 years of age ... his features bore rather a smile than any other expression.[6]

*The Standard*:

> [Corder] appears about twenty-four years of age ... appearing sulking and ill-tempered.[7]

The following narrative uses Curtis's account as the primary source, cross-checked against the newspapers for accuracy;

---

[*]  See Appendix 4.

[†]  It should have been 'enveloping' membrane.

where clarification or amplification is required – or Curtis gets it wrong – the alternative source will be identified. In reading the press reports some of the facts are virtually impossible to disentangle, mainly in respect of the medical evidence, and these will be noted in the text.

Mr Andrews rose to make the opening statement for the prosecution; the report of his speech occupied twelve pages in Curtis's book. Since it repeated evidence from the inquest, and all the facts would again be examined as witnesses were called, it is sufficient to say that he summarized the details of the case and declared that the body found in the barn would be identified as belonging to Maria Martin.

Ann Martin, Maria's stepmother, was the first witness for the prosecution; she was examined by Mr Andrews. Ann Martin had known William Corder for seventeen years; she described in detail William and Maria's relationship, which started in earnest on or before May 1826, the baby born at Sudbury, the missing five-pound note and their arguments about it and the surreptitious burial of the baby. She described how they had left for Ipswich via the Red Barn to get married, what Maria was wearing and why she was disguised. At some point, she said that Corder had shown her a gold ring purchased in Colchester that was to be Maria's wedding ring. Corder had a loaded gun with him when they left for the Red Barn. She related how her son had spotted Corder later in the afternoon with a pickaxe over his shoulder although Corder later denied that it was him. She had never received a letter from Maria after she left, because, Corder said, Maria had a bad hand. When she asked Corder what Maria would do for changes of clothes, he told her that 'Miss Rowland' with whom Maria was staying had plenty that would fit her. She mentioned a handkerchief that Maria had with her that belonged to her little boy; Corder said it was lost. She described how she saw Corder with Maria's umbrella at his brother's funeral. Initially Corder denied it was Maria's, but later conceded that it was and Maria had lent it to him. She described Maria's physical appearance; she had a wen on her neck* and a tooth missing from either jaw. She also had a cough of long duration.

Mr Brodrick rose to cross-examine Mrs Martin, and in response to his questions she added further details: she had three children; Maria was her stepdaughter and had a sister and brother from Ann's husband's previous marriage. She commented on the relationship between William and Maria:

> I was anxious that Maria should marry the prisoner, but I do not know that she was anxious about it.

She said that Maria was two months† in Sudbury; the prisoner brought her home with the child which subsequently died in her (Ann's) arms. 'They' took it away after a day and two nights and

> I do not know that it was buried at Sudbury. After the child was taken from my home, I knew nothing about it.

Mr Brodrick:

> Now, woman, on your solemn oath, do you know that it was not buried at Sudbury, but that you know when and where it was buried?

Ann Martin:

> Maria always told me that it was buried at Sudbury, that is all I know about it.

Mr Brodrick:

> Do you not know that, instead of going to Sudbury, Maria went to Mr Corder's house, and slept there?

Ann Martin:

---

\* This was probably a sebaceous cyst.

† Evidence from Maria's landlady at Sudbury suggested that it was one month.

The prisoner told me she was there.

Mr Brodrick:

When was that?

Ann Martin:

When he came home with her. Maria was present when he said so. From what they both told me, I had reason to believe that they had not been to Sudbury.

She said that Maria's sister, Ann, and Mrs Martin's 'little boy', George, were at home when Corder and Maria left and were aware that they were going to the barn. She mentioned Corder's pistols; he would 'snap' them in the fireplace. He gave her money for Maria's little boy after they went away. She said there had been 'talk' among other people about Maria being 'taken up' for her bastard children; she was sure Corder had told Maria this. She mentioned her examination by Mr Wayman under oath, both at the inquest and afterwards. She said that Maria used to dress 'rather fine', causing quarrels between her, Maria, Maria's sister Ann and her father. Finally she said that Maria was 'very dull' when she went away on 18 May. In response to a question from Mr Andrews, Mrs Martin said that she supposed the money Corder gave her for the support of Maria's little boy came from Maria.

It is most surprising that Brodrick did not mention the question of the body being found as a consequence of Ann Martin's dreams, and did not subject her to any cross-examination on the subject. Curtis commented that Ann Martin appeared to be a 'decently dressed countrywoman'; the prisoner put his spectacles on and 'looked steadfastly at her.' She never returned the look. There was a rumour circulating, Curtis said, that the Corder family had 'bought off' Ann Martin, but he observed:

during the long enquiry and the following rigid cross-examination, no person could give her evidence more satisfactorily.

It was the turn of Ann's husband Thomas Martin next. He said that Maria and William Corder had been intimate for about a year and a half before they went away. He repeated some of what his wife had already told the court. He searched the Red Barn on 19 April 1828 'in consequence of what my wife used to say to me.' He and Mr Pryke, Mrs Corder's bailiff, examined one of the bays which was covered with 'litter and fodder':

> He raked and I poked into the straw a good while before we found anything … I found some large loose stones about the middle of the bay … there was an appearance of the earth having been disturbed. When I had poked with my mole-spike about four inches, I found something came out with it like flesh. I smelt of it and it was very disagreeable. We made further search, and found that the hole contained a body.

Pryke said they ought to get someone else before they went any further, and eventually came back with Mr Bowtell. They further excavated around the body and found the handkerchief around the neck.

> The body was … not stretched out. The hole appeared to be about three feet or three feet and a half long. The legs were drawn up, and the head bent down. I put my mole-spike near the hip-bone; the spike is about as thick as my little finger.

Having discovered the body, they left it there until the next day when the inquest was held. The earth was cleared from the body and it was removed from the hole and placed on a door to be taken to the light and examined:

> I could not swear to the body, but the face and mouth looked like my daughter's. She had a wen about her gullet; she had had a stoppage in her throat for some time, and a bad cough.

He found a busk, earrings, part of a pair of stays, a shift and some combs, which were subsequently given to the constable.

Thomas Martin was cross-examined by Mr Brodrick; he said they tried several times with the handle of the rake before they found anything and 'I am sure it was about the hip of the body where I put my spike in.' He confirmed that he was examined by Mr Wayman at the Cock Inn with no magistrate present; the prisoner was also not present.

Maria's sister, Ann Martin junior, was examined next. She was 21 years old, and Thomas Martin's youngest daughter with his first wife Grace. She confirmed what her stepmother and father had said about the circumstances of Maria's departure and what William Corder had subsequently told them. She was present at the inquest and saw the body removed from the Red Barn; she knew it to be her sister's from 'the things she had on', describing these in great detail, also by her 'teeth, her mouth and her features generally.' She added that the men's clothes, which Maria donned to avoid being recognized on her way to the Red Barn, had belonged to William's brother, James Corder. She was cross-examined by Mr Prendergast; she said that Maria was very low spirited and crying when she left home, adding:

> I am not aware that my sister wanted to marry the prisoner, but I have heard her say she should marry him. William Corder used to say that he was going to be married to her, but Maria did not say the same thing frequently.

She said that she, Maria, and their stepmother quarrelled occasionally; 'they might have angry words sometimes, but not very often.'

Next to be examined was George Martin, Maria's ten-year-old half-brother. He was first questioned by the judge.

Judge:

> How old are you, my little fellow?

George Martin:

> About ten years old.

Judge:

> Do you know the nature of an oath? What will become of you when you die, if you swear falsely, and state the things that are not true?

George Martin:

> God would send me to hell, Sir.

Judge:

> Let him be sworn.

George Martin was examined by Mr Kelly. He said that Maria was his sister; he saw her the day she left with William Corder, at half-past twelve, and on that day:

> [Corder] had a gun with him, which, I heard him say was loaded ... He had nothing, as I saw, but the gun when he went out ... It was half past twelve when my sister went out, and this is the last time in my life I ever saw her

But on the same day:

> I saw [Corder] again coming from the barn with a pickaxe on his shoulder ... it was about half past three when I saw him ... going from the Red Barn homewards ... in Broadfield ... he went across Broadfield, and came over the corner of it, and went into Thistley Lay, in the way which led to his own house ... I was in Wellfield, and it is likely he did not see me ... I was only about 20 roods [sic] from him ... cutting up grass for my dickey [donkey].

The report in the *Standard* said 20 *rods*, and this was probably what was meant.[*] Thus George Martin was about 110 yards or 100 metres from William Corder when he saw him. George Martin was not cross-examined.

Next on the stand was Phoebe Stow who lived about '30 rods'[†] from the Red Barn. Her house was the nearest one to the Red Barn. Phoebe Stow had known Corder for years, and the previous summer she remembered lending him her husband's spade. He had said that he was in a hurry and couldn't stop to talk. She remembered approximately when it was, because she had been 'confined' on 29 April, and 'churched' exactly four weeks later. She thought that the day she lent him the spade was 'a little more than a week' before her churching. She then repeated a later conversation she had with William Corder around harvest time. She had asked him about the child Maria had had at Sudbury; he told her it was dead and buried and that Maria would 'never have any more'. The conversation continued:

Phoebe Stow:

> She is a young woman, and may have many more children yet.

William Corder:

> No, Maria Martin will never be troubled with any more children.

Phoebe Stow:

> What do you go by?

William Corder:

> She has had her number.

---

\* A rod is 5½ yards, a *rood* was 'originally the same as a rod ... but in later use usually either seven or eight yards' *OED*.

† 165 yards or 150 metres

Phoebe Stow:

> That neither you or I can tell.

William Corder:

> I can for I'll be damned if she will have any more.

Phoebe Stow:

> [You say that you are married to Maria Martin, why don't you live with her?]

William Corder:

> She is where I can go to her at any day or hour I please.

Phoebe Stow:

> Perhaps you are rather jealous and think that when you are away, she is with somebody else.

William Corder:

> When I am away, I am sure nobody else is with her.

Mrs Stow was cross-examined by Mr Brodrick and generated a laugh in court by saying: 'I am not a gossiping woman, or more talkative than most women generally are.' She was not, she said, aware that Corder was managing his mother's farm; she may have lent spades to 'some of the men ... at a "chance time"'. She was not examined on the conversation she had had with Corder at the inquest, but sworn later 'by Mr Wayman'. Mr Kelly took up the cross-examination; she added:

> When I was examined before the coroner, I do not remember that anybody put a question to me about the conversation I had with Corder. Nothing was asked of me, except about the spade.

Then, following a question by Mr Brodrick, 'There is another cottage joins mine, and another between a quarter and half a mile from the Red Barn.'

The next witness was Rachael *Burke,* (Curtis), *Bugg* (*The Standard*) or *Buck* (*The Times*). The Prosecution Brief called her 'Rachael Bugg' so that was probably her name. She lived in 'the farmhouse', almost certainly the Corder farmhouse; Corder came to her and said: 'Maria Martin would not be your mistress, as she was gone over to France in a steam-packet.' The implication being, that if Corder had married Maria and brought her to live with him in the family house, Rachael Bugg, who worked there, would have been her servant.

William Martin, Maria's cousin, was examined next. His evidence was somewhat muted compared with what he had sworn in the 3 June depositions. Having asked about Maria, Corder had said that she was not living in Sudbury, but that 'I can see her any time I please'. They were near Corder's house, he gave Martin some beer to drink and told him not to talk too loud in case people in the house overheard their conversation.

Now it was the turn of Francis Stow, Phoebe's husband. He was a farm labourer who worked on the Corders' harvest the previous summer and was paid by William Corder. He described how the first load of corn was put into that part of the Red Barn where the body was found, although he was unaware of any orders on the subject given by Corder. He related how one day, at harvest time, Corder had come to him and offered him, smiling, a one-pound note to cut his (Corder's) throat. He was cross-examined by Mr Brodrick and said that his wife never told him about the borrowed spade 'nor did he miss it'. Then:

> I never said anything about the one-pound note until I heard about this matter. I was never examined more than once previous to my coming before the grand jury.

William Martin was recalled by Mr Brodrick and said:

> I was not examined before the coroner's jury – never, indeed, before I came here, either before a magistrate or otherwise.

It is clear from the defence questions about previous examinations that they were rattled by the new, to them, evidence from Phoebe Stow, Rachael Bugg and William Martin, which from subsequent comments, had not been made available to them beforehand. They had only seen Phoebe Stow's evidence from the inquest on the borrowing of the spade, and nothing of that of Rachael Bugg or William Martin. What Mrs Stow had to say about her conversation with William Corder was most damaging to the defence case as was the evidence of William Martin, which was listed in the Prosecution Brief, undated, and therefore likely, as he said, not sworn to before a magistrate. Rachael Bugg's evidence was also not given at the inquest, and added another layer to William's lies about Maria's whereabouts.

William Towns was next on the stand. He had been a labourer for many years in the employ of the Corder family. He assisted in filling the right-hand bay of the Red Barn where the body was found with wheat from America Hill field, on the orders of William Corder. He added that wheat had been put into that bay for years. The corn that was put in the previous year, 'was thrashed out before Stoke Fair which begins on the 16 May'. He had done it himself, beginning in February and finishing in March. He cleared the sheaves away and lay straw in the right hand bay. He did not 'remove the litter so as to see the ground'. Cross-examined by Mr Brodrick, he added that he had known William Corder for eighteen years. Being asked by Brodrick whether he was a kind-hearted young man, Towns said:

> I never saw him out of temper; he was very good to me indeed. I have laboured for his family for 18 years.

William Pryke was examined next. He described himself as 'farming bailiff' to Mrs Corder, although he was effectively managing the farm in William's absence. He related the occasion 'on or about 18 September [1827]', when he drove the prisoner to Colchester:

> While we were going along, I had a conversation with him respecting the business ... as I was about to take management of the farm

He said that Corder told him he had not seen Maria since May; he spoke 'very highly' of her but said no more. He was with Thomas Martin when the body was discovered, 'lying on its right side doubled up'. It was he who had discovered the body and he used his rake to remove the earth. He was in the barn the next day for the inquest; he had locked the barn overnight and kept the keys with him. The body was in the same state the next day as it was when they discovered it.

He was cross-examined by Mr Brodrick. He commented that when he drove Corder to Colchester, Corder had been ill for some time with a doctor in attendance. Corder said Maria was 'a well-deserving girl in terms of tender affection.' Pryke was at the inquest the whole day, he said, but was not questioned. Mr Brodrick's indignation boiled over:

> My Lord, this is the most extraordinary case I ever heard of. Is it not strange that such a witness as this should not be examined before the coroner? Who, by the way, I ought to mention refused to allow the attendance of the prisoner during the inquest over which he (Mr Wayman) presided; so ... that my client is put ... upon his trial, and for the first time to hear the evidence adduced against him. How ... is a man so circumstanced to defend himself against accusations which involve not his liberty, but his life?

Judge:

> Is it not very unusual for the prisoner to be excluded on such occasions?

Mr Brodrick:

> Very unusual, indeed, my Lord! And it is, likewise, very unusual for a coroner, who sat in such a cause to conduct the prosecution afterwards, as an attorney for the prosecution against the prisoner, who had been so excluded.

He continued:

> Most unusual, too, is it ... that the Coroner, while acting as such attorney, should, himself, in a private room, without the prisoner's having any notice of it, examine the witnesses on oath, and collect their evidence, no magistrate being present.

Mr Wayman, the coroner/prosecutor rose and stated that the prisoner had been attended by Mr Humphreys who was:

> a very respectable solicitor, from London; and it was by that gentleman's request that the prisoner did not stop in the room to hear the depositions read over to him.

This was clever obfuscation by Mr Wayman. It had happened exactly as he described, and Humphreys was to read the depositions to Corder afterwards, but it was only the depositions made in the inquest. The subsequent ones, sworn on 27 May and 3 June, together with the four that were undated, neither the prisoner nor the defence team had ever seen.

Mr Brodrick responded:

> We have no evidence of that fact: we have not got Mr Humphreys here to prove it.

Mr Andrews resumed his examination of William Pryke, who stated that he was examined and sworn by Mr Wayman, at the Cock Inn, with no magistrate present.[*] He finished by saying that William Corder was a kind-hearted young man. Mr Brodrick then asked:

Pray, sir, had you not got a person preaching about this murder, in or near this very barn?

Judge:

What do you mean by preaching – is it a sermon you allude to?

Mr Brodrick:

Yes, my Lord, and to a congregation of several thousands of persons, which were specially brought together, after regular notice in the parish, to hear the prisoner at the bar described as the murderer of this unfortunate girl.

Judge:

You do not mean a clergyman of the Church of England?

Mr Brodrick:

No, my Lord, I understand it was a dissenter. Pray, Mr Pryke, what was the name of this preacher?

William Pryke:

I understood his name was Young and he came from London.

Mr Brodrick:

This is not all, my Lord – for in the very neighbourhood, and, indeed, in all parts of the country, there have been puppet-shows, representing this catastrophe.

Mr Andrews now chimed in, no doubt having been talking to Wayman:

---

[*]   This was the examination on 3 June

> I wish to say a few words in respect to the conduct of the coroner.

Mr Brodrick:

> I object my Lord, to my learned friend being heard, unless he produces the coroner as a witness, and to that I can have no objection.

But the judge did; it was nothing to do with the trial, he said, there was

> enough to do without it. It may be an imputation upon the character of the Coroner, perhaps; but we are not sitting in judgement to try whether it be just or unjustly founded.

Mr Andrews sought to clarify:

> It was arranged between the coroner and Mr Humphreys … that though Corder was not allowed to be present at the inquest, the depositions were afterwards read to him. I believe, my Lord, that is the usual practice on these occasions.

Mr Prendergast did not agree:

> The practice is directly the contrary, and so are the words of Lord Coke*

William Chaplin was examined next; he was 'overseer of Polstead' and produced the two letters Corder had written to Thomas Martin. Brodrick said to him: 'As well as being churchwarden of Polstead, are you not the prosecutor in this cause?' He replied that he was.

---

* Sir Edward Coke was a notable seventeenth-century lawyer and politician who wrote extensively on the law and was largely responsible for the passing of the Petition of Right at the time of Charles I. 'Coke's works have been to the common law what Shakespeare has been to literature and the King James Bible to religion.' *ODNB*

Mr Brodrick:

Did you hear the parson preach in or near the barn?

Mr Chaplin:

No, certainly not, but I heard of the occurrence.

Mr Brodrick:

And you took no steps to prevent it?

Mr Chaplin:

No, I did not.

Mr Brodrick:

Are there not exhibitions going about the neighbourhood, representing Corder as the murderer?

Mr Chaplin:

I have heard so.

Mr Brodrick:

And you have not interfered to prevent them. Is there not a camera obscura near this very hall at this moment exhibiting him as the murderer?

Mr Chaplin:

There is a camera obscura, I believe, about the streets, but I do not know the nature of the exhibition; neither am I aware that I have any power to prevent them in my own parish, much less in this town.

Thomas Martin was recalled and proved that the two letters supplied by William Chaplin were the ones he had received from William Corder. These were the letters, previously mentioned, dated October 1827, and were read out in court. In the first one, Corder says that he and Maria had married, that she had sent her father a letter with all the details, and that she was surprised not to have heard from him; furthermore, he should burn all of their correspondence. The second letter expresses surprise that Maria's letter to her father was never received, and says that they (William and Maria) have to avoid falling into 'Mr P's' hands etc. and they are unable to return to Polstead.

Mr P, Peter Mathews, was the next to give evidence, being examined by Mr Andrews. He said that he generally lived in London, but that he had relatives in Polstead. He knew William Corder and had known Maria Martin for some time; he last saw her on 31 August 1826. He was in Polstead in the summer of 1827 and had a conversation with Corder about Maria and the missing five-pound note. He said that in response to his questions, '[Corder] answered falsely'.

Mr Brodrick:

Sir, you must state the conversation and not the result.

Peter Mathews described the conversation he had had with Corder over the money, which Corder initially denied knowing anything about. He referred to one of two letters Corder had written to him; Mr Brodrick commented that the letter was not evidence that it came from the prisoner. The judge noted the objection, but did not think it important. Mathews produced the letter which, he said, he believed to be in Corder's handwriting. George Gardiner, Corder's friend, was called and 'reluctantly' agreed that the letter was in Corder's handwriting. The letter was read:

August 1, 1827.

Sir, – After a long, restless and wretched night of miserable reflections, I have at last endeavoured to collect my weary spirits, in order to fulfil your request

At this point Mr Brodrick rose and said that the letter had no reference to the offence with which the prisoner was charged. The judge agreed saying 'let the letter lie on the table for the present'. The letter in question has been described in an earlier chapter. Stripped of the grovelling obsequiousness, Corder admits to the 'enormous crime' – not directly mentioned, but clearly referring to the theft of the five-pound note – and throws himself on Peter Mathews' mercy. The second letter from Corder to Mathews was read out in court in full. This was the letter in which Corder acknowledged Mathews' 'forgiveness' for the theft, and then proceeded to spin a web of falsehood over Maria Martin's whereabouts, her reasons for being unable to write and conversations he had with her. The letter finished by promising to enclose a letter from Mathews to Maria along with one of his own.

Peter Mathews' reply was also read out. This was dated 2 September. In it he asked for Maria's address so that he could write to her directly. He said he wanted to be a 'friend to all', that is, Maria, Corder and his family, and offered them friendly counsel. Peter Mathews' examination continued. Mr Brodrick asked him whether Maria Martin was 'in any way' concerned with the five-pound note, but the judge thought it was rather 'straining the case' and the matter was dropped. Mathews described a conversation he had with Corder in early August of 1827 regarding Maria's whereabouts. Corder said he 'would forward it if he could'. Corder mentioned 'something about Brentford'.* Mathews said:

> I told him I must insist upon his forwarding the letter, as there appeared to be a great deal of concealment in the business.

---

* Mathews must have been confused here. It was several months later that Corder moved to Brentford, after Mrs Ingleton had responded to the Corders' advertisement.

Corder then told him that he believed Maria to be 'somewhere near Yarmouth'. Mathews described the chance meeting he had with Corder near Somerset House in London on 19 November 1827. He asked Corder if he had forwarded the letter he had given him for Maria. Corder said that he had, but Mathews said he was surprised not to have received an answer. He asked where Maria was and was told that he had 'left her on the Isle of Wight'. He told Corder that her father had written to him once or twice respecting Maria, 'they were uneasy, not knowing where she was'. He said 'Are you married to her yet?' He replied that he was not as he had not settled his affairs yet.

Next on the stand was the redoubtable James Lea who had arrested Corder in Brentford. He described how Corder was traced to Ealing and how he had denied three times that he knew Maria Martin. On their way to the Red Lion in Brentford, Lea told him that the body of a young woman had been discovered. Initially he made no reply, but then just asked when the discovery had been made. Lea then went back to the house and opened some 'writing desks' upstairs with keys he had taken from Corder. Mr Brodrick seemed to be struggling, because his next interjection was rather weak:

> There is not proof that the desks were his; the mere fact of some keys being taken ... ought not to be given in evidence; it is no assumption that they were his. If the prisoner had been by at the time and acknowledged them to have been so, the case would have been otherwise.

The judge observed: 'It was his house, or place of abode, where they were found'. Mr Andrews said he would 'obviate the difficulty'. James Lea continued; he said:

> I had some conversation with the prisoner respecting some pistols which I found at his house. When I was taking him from Polstead to Bury gaol, he said he would

present them to me. He said he bought them at Ipswich when he was ten years of age.

Lea said that he found the pistols in a black velvet bag hanging on a nail in the 'dressing-room at the house in Ealing'. The pistols were produced but 'immediately put by'. Curtis wrote that at this point:

> the noise and confusion outside the court was so great, that the business was suspended for a few minutes until the javelin-men went out to quell the riot, with an order to bring the offenders before the judge, who said he would certainly commit them to prison.

Lea continued; he said that Corder's offer to give him the pistols was made after he (Lea) had made his deposition to the coroner, which was then read to Corder, along with the other depositions.

At some point during James Lea's examination on the question of the pistols, Curtis reported that Corder violently stamped his foot, muttering under his breath that 'Lea would swear any thing.' Mr Andrews called for the pistols to be produced; Mr Brodrick was not happy:

> I object to them being produced, as they do not appear to be the prisoner's, or that they were found at his house – *non constat*\* that the house was the house of the prisoner, there being other persons living in it.

Judge:

> Were they and the prisoner in the room at the same time?

Lea:

> Yes, my Lord.

---

\*   Non constat – it is doubted or it is not certain.

Judge:

> I think I should be straining the point very far if I were to reject this evidence; besides the prisoner made the pistols his own, or treated them as his own property, when he offered to make a present of them to Lea.

Mr Brodrick:

> My Lord, we only have Lea's evidence that such an offer was made; and without intending the slightest imputation on his veracity, he is an interested witness.

The pistols were produced; Mr Andrews:

> Mr Lea, did you not afterwards find a sword at the prisoner's house in Ealing?

Mr Brodrick:

> Do you mean to press that question?

Mr Andrews:

> Of course I do.

Mr Brodrick:

> Then I'll raise my objection at once; and I must refer again to the pistols.

Judge:

> Were the pistols at the coroner's inquest?

Lea:

> Yes.

Mr Brodrick:

> Ay, but the prisoner was not there to see them.

Lea:

> I think he must have known that I had them, because
> they lay about the room all the time I had him in custody.

Judge:

> Let the witness proceed.

Lea:

> I found this powder-flask, bullet-mould, and these
> bullets, with the pistol, in the bag. When I took the
> prisoner, I saw a sword hanging on a nail. After the
> prisoner was committed, I went again to Ealing, but now
> it had been removed; but I found it, and have it now in
> my possession.

Mr Andrews said he would not produce it (the sword) yet,
but called Mr Robert Offord who was examined by Mr Kelly.
Offord was a cutler from Hadleigh; he was acquainted with
Corder. Around March or April 1827, the prisoner brought him
a small sword that he wanted 'ground as sharp as a carving
knife'. He said he had a cousin 'about to marry' and he wanted
the sword ground the same day. He said he thought he would
know the sword again. James Lea produced the sword which
was hanging from a white military belt. He continued:

> I found this in the dressing room, the second time I went
> to Ealing; the same room that I took the reticule from – it
> was in a trunk in the room.

Robert Offord was recalled and identified the sword as the one
Corder had given him to grind: 'I know it by my own work'. He
ground it quite sharp and Corder collected it in the evening: 'I
am quite confident that this is the same sword'.

Curtis noted that the sword was 'about two feet in
length' well-polished, and the shape of an 'imperfect crescent',
although Offord had said in his deposition at the inquest, that
it was a 'scimitar blade ... twelve to thirteen inches long'.

Mr Brodrick now asked a very odd question:

> You have said that it was in March or early in April last
> year that you ground the sword: mind, I warn you well,
> you swear that it was not before Christmas 1826.*

Robert Offord:

> I will not. I do not keep a job-book. I have been speaking
> by guess as to the time, and to the best of my recollection.
> I know I was working in the shop by candle-light when
> he called for it.

Mr Brodrick:

> Well, but you work with candles at Christmas as well as
> March?

Robert Offord:

> Certainly ... I know I was in the shop when the prisoner
> came for it. There were no marks upon the blade when
> he took it away. I perceive there are now two or three
> stains, and something like a scratch ... I will not positively
> swear that the spots near the point were not on it when
> I gave it to Corder, but there was no scratch.

Mr Andrews recalled George Gardiner; he had seen a sword
like it at Mrs Corder's house at Polstead.

He was cross-examined by Mr Brodrick. There had been
an 'alarm' and they were worried that Mrs Corder's house had
been targeted for robbery:

> Corder had this sword in his room. We sat up several
> nights, as there had been several robberies in the
> neighbourhood.

Mr Kelly now called John Baalham, constable of Polstead. He
knew Corder and Maria Martin well; he never had a warrant

---

* It was never made clear what the significance of 'Christmas 1826' was.

to arrest her. On being cross-examined by Mr Brodrick he said: 'there was a report about the place that she would be taken up.' The matter had, apparently, been discussed at a parish meeting, but since Maria had not applied for parochial relief, there would have been no justification for doing so. Baalham had known the prisoner all his life; he lived only 40 rods from his house. He said: 'I can give him the character of a kind-hearted, good-tempered young man.'

Mr Kelly called Henry Harcourt, a gunmaker from Sudbury who also knew Corder.* In February 1827 Corder brought him a pair of pistols for repair:

> I cannot say whether the pistols now produced are the same, but I know they were percussion pistols, similar to those. Percussion pistols have been in vogue seven or eight years.

Judge:

> In vogue you say; how long have they been invented?

Henry Harcourt:

> I should think it is seven or eight years since I first saw anything of the kind.

Mr Brodrick:

> I suppose you are a county gun-maker, then?

Henry Harcourt:

> Yes I am. When Corder took them away, a young woman was with him, but I did not know her. She was not with him when he brought them. I never saw her call alone respecting them.

---

\* It is a minor oddity that the Ipswich maker of the pistols was also a 'Harcourt'. They may have been related, or it may just have been coincidence; neither Curtis nor anyone else commented on it.

Thomas Akers was now examined by Mr Andrews. Corder had said that it was him that George Martin had seen with a pickaxe over his shoulder on the afternoon that Corder and Maria had left. He lived in Polstead during May of the previous year, and knew the Red Barn and Thistley Lay. He denied that about the time of Stoke Fair (16 April) he was ever 'across the Lay or a field near it with a pickaxe on my shoulder, or at any other time.' And he had not been planting trees for Mr Hoy on Hoy's hill. He was cross-examined by Mr Brodrick:

> I was at work in the neighbourhood of Polstead at that time, but I do not know what I was doing. I almost always worked with horses. I do not know whether, in the course of last year, I worked with a pickaxe at all.

He did, however, admit to wearing a velveteen jacket, as did William Corder sometimes.

It was now the turn of Mr John Lawton, the Boxford surgeon who was present at the barn with the coroner's jury, and had overseen the raising of the body on Sunday 20 April 1828. Lawton was 29 years old. He had been apprenticed at the age of 15 to Mr Mudd of Gedding with whom he spent six years; Gedding was around ten miles north of Polstead. Lawton had also spent time in London and although he had 'seen dead bodies dissected', he had no experience of a body that had been buried for so long. When he arrived at the barn the body had not been lifted from the hole, but the earth had been removed from the top of it:

> It lay in a hole in the barn, where it had been buried, and was covered with straw when I first went in. It was in the further, or right bay of the barn, as I went in from the yard. The body was then very much decomposed; but some parts more than others ... I should have said it had lain nine or ten months in the ground...

He proceeded to list the items of clothing found on the body, some of which were produced:

There was [also] the sleeve of a blue coat. The body was put into a sack, pieces of which I took off the body. The body was lying on its right side ... she was quite crowded down ... I examined the face, which was in a very bad state, and there was an appearance of blood about it on the right cheek. I found this striped handkerchief round the neck. It was drawn extremely tight, so as to form a complete groove round the neck. It was apparently done for the purpose, as if pulled by some person. It was drawn sufficiently tight to have ... produced strangulation. A man's hand might pass between the exterior and interior fold of the handkerchief. In the neck, I discovered the appearance of a stab about an inch in length and perpendicular. I passed my finger through the wound, and found that it descended to the left side; but I cannot say what parts were particularly injured by it, the part was in so putrid a state. There was a wen about the middle of the neck; it is an enlargement of the gland, but the common people call it a "wen". There was an appearance of an injury having been done to the right eye, and the right side of the face apparently. I think it was done in two ways. It appeared as if something had passed into the eye deep into the orbit, injuring the bone on the right side of the nose. It [also] appeared as if it had been done by something having passed through the left cheek, and then passing out through the right orbit; and there was also a stab in the right eye. It appeared to me as if a ball had passed through the left cheek, removing the last two grinders. The brain of the deceased was in such a state that I could make nothing out of it ... The bone which divides the nostril was completely removed

111

out of its place and broken to pieces, apparently by a ball having passed through.

However:

I do not think that a ball passing through as I have stated would have produced death. Not instant death of itself; but strangulation, and the stab in the neck, together with the ball would, if all concurring together.

So according to Mr Lawton, Maria had been shot through the face, stabbed in the neck and eye and strangled with a handkerchief. He then went on to describe his examination of the rest of the body:

I opened the chest of the deceased, but I did not discover any injury there myself.

There was an 'adhesion of the lungs' which would cause coughing; Maria was known to have had a cough. After describing the advanced state of decomposition of the body, he reiterated his views on the cause of death:

the injury round the neck inflicted with the handkerchief would have caused death, but not the wounds without it, except from subsequent inflammation. They would not have caused instant death; but I will not speak positively.

He went on to say that he had only examined the body once; he was away when it was exhumed. He did have the head in his possession (which he had removed on the day of the inquest), and the heart and ribs had been brought to him by Mr Nairn who was present during the exhumation along with Mr Chaplin:

Upon my subsequent inspection, I found something had penetrated between the fifth and sixth ribs, and there was a stab in the heart which exactly corresponded with the wound in the ribs ... that injury alone would have been, in my opinion, sufficient ... to produce death.

There was a cut in the shift, he said, which corresponded with those in the ribs and heart; nothing could be seen in the stays which were too decayed. The 'short sword' (Corder's sword) 'exactly' fitted the wound, as well as the wound in the sphenoidal sinus which it penetrated about a quarter of an inch.* He went on:

I have examined the wound in the head, and compared it with a bullet.

Judge:

Then was a bullet found in the wound?

Mr Brodrick:

Nothing of the sort, my Lord.

Mr Andrews sought to clarify:

My Lord, it is the bullet found by Lea in the reticule.

Judge:

What in the Red Barn?

Mr Andrews:

No, my Lord, at Ealing, in the bag which contained the pistols.

Mr Lawton continued:

The bullet fitted the hole, and as I passed it through it, it appeared to have been perforated with a ball of that size. I think the ball was fired before the stab with the

---

* The sphenoidal sinus is a cavity in the skull more or less behind the eye, and by inference, the wound was a consequence of the 'stab in the right eye'.

sharp instrument. My reason for thinking so is, because I consider that the ball alone would not have killed her; but I could not tell this from any appearance of the body: it is my own opinion only.

He went on to describe how he had found blood on the stays, the shift, the handkerchief around the neck and another handkerchief. The lower and upper jaw had each lost a tooth. He then produced the skull in court to show the missing teeth; a further tooth had subsequently been lost.

Under cross-examination from Mr Brodrick, he admitted that he did not observe the stab in the ribs, 'or the pistol bullet' during his examination of the body during the inquest. Having observed that the body was 'not so much decomposed as might have been expected', he said that the face, hands and feet, were very decomposed. However, in spite of the putrefaction in the face, he could see that 'the wound gaped', indicating that it had been made in life. Mr Brodrick wanted to know how he could tell whether a wound had been made before or after death. Mr Lawton:

wounds inflicted in life gape open, which is not the case when made in putrid flesh.

He admitted that he had made a wound on the heart when he opened the chest on the day of the inquest, a wound on the right ventricle; this was not the wound apparently made by stabbing, which was 'near the apex of the heart between the right and left ventricle'. He saw no other injuries, and none that could have been made with a spade. The mark of the handkerchief around the neck could, he said, have been made if the body had been 'raise[d] up' by someone lifting or pulling the body by the handkerchief. Mr Brodrick pressed him on the stab wound subsequently discovered between the ribs:

When I took the shift from the body I saw no mark on it; it was produced at the Cock at Polstead [the inquest].

> I did not look for it [the mark] till I had discovered the wound in the heart and ribs.

Then:

> I can't tell whether they were there or made afterwards, of my own knowledge. I did not see them, although I examined the body.

He insisted that his judgement was based on his own opinion and not affected by anything he had heard since. On the question of the direction of the pistol shot to the face:

> I can speak with certainty that the ball came out of the eye, from the manner in which the bones are driven in. I can tell what course the ball would take. The bones were very much shattered

He said that at the inquest he had been unable to tell from his initial inspection of the body whether this was the result of a 'pistol bullet' or decomposition. Mr Kelly then re-examined the witness. He had seen the dissection of many dead bodies, and was able to distinguish between wounds made before and after death:

> I believe none of the wounds to which I have spoken were done when the body was dug up.

He did not particularly examine the hips of the body.* He reiterated that the groove round the neck caused by the handkerchief might have been caused 'if the body had been lifted up by the fold of the handkerchief soon after death'. He said that different parts of the body were in different stages of decomposition, the wrists and feet were particularly badly decomposed. On the wound to the head he was in no doubt; after cleaning the bones it was clear that '[it] was done with a bullet at some time or other'.

---

*   This was where Thomas Martin thought he might have thrust his mole-spike.

Mr Andrews now proposed to call another medical witness to corroborate Mr Lawton's testimony. He would also call witnesses to identify Maria Martin's clothes and thus prove that the body found in the Red Barn was hers, but the judge had had enough for the day:

> I think, in such a case as this, the hour has arrived when we ought to adjourn the Court, as it is quite evident that we cannot finish the trial tonight.

There was more prosecution evidence to be heard, there was also the defence case and the judge's 'charge' to the jury (the summing-up). In view of the lateness of the hour, around half-past six in the evening, and a trial of such 'solemn importance' to the prisoner and the public, with everyone fatigued, the judge declared the court adjourned until the next day. There was a minor comedy when one of the sheriff's officers initially refused to be sworn to attend a jury member during the night; this was needed in order to prevent communication on the case with anyone. Having been threatened with a fine if he failed to comply he was duly sworn and the court adjourned at a quarter to seven.

The court reconvened on Friday 8 August. The organized chaos of the previous morning was not repeated, Mr Orridge having instructed the sheriff's officers to keep the 'avenues of the court' clear:

> the public were this day afforded every reasonable accommodation ... a great number of ladies obtained admission to witness

According to *The Standard*, it was the High Sheriff, Mr Hart Logan, who had 'interfered personally' to prevent a recurrence of the 'disgraceful scenes' of the previous day. The newspaper observed:

To-day the court presents a very different aspect from yesterday, and a fair proportion of those assembled are respectable persons. The consequence of the conduct pursued yesterday was, that the respectable part of society were put in peril of their lives, and the stout, able-bodied, but lawless personages of the lowest rank, over-rode every obstacle that could be opposed to them, and rushed in and filled the court.[8]

William Corder was 'put to the bar' at a quarter to nine, where having put on his spectacles, he sighed deeply, leaning against a pillar of the court building, according to Curtis, 'oscillating and swinging ... his body'. The judge took his seat at nine o'clock, and having made 'polite obeisance to the ladies who occupied other parts of the court than the bench', proceedings began.

Mr Andrews called another surgeon, John Charles Nairn. He had been present when Maria's body was exhumed on 19 May. Nairn had been in practice for a year, with around twelve years in the profession. He had 'examined the cavities of the chest'. Mr Brodrick interrupted; he wanted the judge to direct that the disinterred body be properly identified. The judge assented and Mr Andrews called John Baalham the parish clerk and constable of Polstead. Baalham confirmed that he had screwed the coffin lid down on the body that had been removed from the Red Barn in the presence of the rector of Polstead, Mr Whitmore. Baalham was not present at the burial, having been called to the coroner at the Cock Inn, although he identified the exhumed coffin as having been the same one that contained the body removed from the barn. Mr Nairn now described his findings:

The internal parts of the chest I found in a good state of preservation, so much so, that any injury ... by penetrating into it, might have been observed ... the heart was divested of its enveloping membrane ... I discovered a large wound at the back of the right

117

ventricle [of the heart]. It appeared to be a recent wound
... that is my opinion[*] ... in the space between the fifth
and sixth ribs, I discovered a wound ... about three-
quarters of an inch broad. My opinion was, that it was a
wound of long duration, and not one recently inflicted ...
After I returned home, I again examined the heart, when
I discovered a slight wound on the apex corresponding
with the external wound between the ribs. It appeared to
have been inflicted with a sharp instrument ... a dagger
or sword.

William Lea handed him the sword he had removed from the
Corder's house in Ealing; Mr Nairn:

I consider it as the instrument most likely to have
inflicted such a wound ... upon a living body it would ...
have caused death.

He went on to state that the sword corresponded with the
wound between the ribs 'to the extent of two or three inches'
and

there appear to ... be some marks, or discoloration, on
the back of the sword blade, which go to the extent I have
last named ... the wound in the heart ... might certainly
have been made with the point of it

He now came to the head wound:

On ... examining the head ... I traced the progress of a ball
entering into the interior and back part of the upper jaw,
and proceeding to the internal angle of the right eye ... I
should conclude it to be a small pistol ball. This wound
might have caused death or she might have survived it

---

[*] The 'enveloping membrane', the pericardium, was removed by Mr Lawton
on 20 April; he had made the 'large wound at the back of the right ventricle'
in doing so.

Then:

> Upon further examination, I discovered a fissure opening into the sphenoidal sinus, or base of the skull, corresponding with the situation of the vertebrae[*] .... This fissure was occasioned by a sharp instrument; any sharp-pointed instrument would have produced it. It extends about a quarter of an inch into the sphenoidal sinus ... The sword corresponds with the wound in the sphenoidal sinus, and it might have occasioned death.

In answer to a question from Mr Brodrick, he stated that he had examined the body on 19 May, 'about a month after it had been discovered in the barn'. Mr Brodrick wanted to know whether exposure to the air could not have caused further decomposition in the body: Mr Nairn:

> My opinion is that it would not; but I never saw a body before, which had lain so long in the ground.

Judge:

> You mean, you never saw one for the purpose of dissection or examination?

Mr Nairn:

> Yes, my Lord.

Prompted by questions from Mr Brodrick, Mr Nairn reiterated his findings:

> When I examined the heart, I found it divested of the pericardium, and a wound in it.

Mr Andrews:

> And the sword now produced corresponds with it?

---

[*] See later note on the apparent confusion regarding the position of the sphenoidal sinus.

Mr Nairn:

> Yes.

To which Mr Brodrick retorted, 'Yes, and so might a sharp-pointed knife'. Mr Nairn responded:

> The wound was done by an instrument, not by decomposition. Looking merely at the heart, and knowing nothing of the circumstances I have now heard, I should say, that the wound in the right ventricle of the heart was a recent one. I judge partly from the evenness of the edges.

Judge:

> You think the wound you now allude to was a recent and not an ancient wound?

Mr Nairn:

> I do, my Lord.

He went on, following a further question from Mr Brodrick:

> I should have been of [the] opinion, independent of anything but the inspection of the heart itself, that one of the wounds was a recent one, and the other more ancient, because the smaller wound of the two had gaping edges. From the nature of the wound, I do not think that it had been inflicted when the pericardium was removed ... I should be of the opinion, that a wound after death would not have the same appearance as if it was inflicted during life.

And the head:

> The bones of the head were not in the least state of decomposition. The only parts which were out of their places, were those which, in my opinion, arose from wounds inflicted by a bullet. I cannot speak of the face,

**Maria Martin.** The one certainty about this image of Maria Martin is that it cannot be a true likeness of her. She had been dead for more than a year when it was drawn in the summer of 1828. Most likely her sister Ann sat for the portrait; she or others may have advised the artist of differences in their features.

**William Corder.** There exist numerous portraits of William Corder. On the day of the execution, the *Morning Chronicle* commented on print shops in Bury crowded with 'persons purchasing "Portraits of Corder," which bear not the slightest resemblance to the prisoner.' This one, by Charles Hancock, has a note written in ink at the bottom: 'We think the lithographic drawing of William Corder by Mr Charles Hancock is the most correct likeness we have seen. [Signed] John Wayman, Coroner; Timothy R Holmes, Under Sherriff; George Hubbard, Surgeon to the Gaol; George Creed, Surgeon to the Suffolk General Hospital'. Wayman and Holmes would have seen Corder frequently; Holmes countersigned Corder's confession and escorted him to the gallows. Of all the portraits extant, it shows someone most like William Corder as he was described: probably no more than twenty-three years old, slightly built and with a turned-up nose and wearing spectacles.

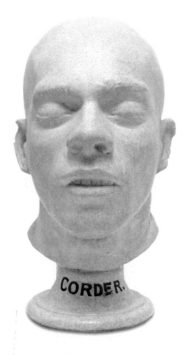

**William Corder's Death Mask.** Two 'artists', Messrs Mizotti and Child, made casts of Corder's head and face more than six hours after he was executed. Observing the body, Curtis noted: 'The countenance did not appear much changed, except that the under lip was drawn down to expose the teeth ... obliterating the indentation ... on the top of the chin.' It is difficult to reconcile this death mask with any of the published images of William Corder, particularly the one endorsed by Wayman and Holmes. This may have been due to the inevitable changes brought on by the violent death and partial dissection of the body, in addition to which the art of Mizotti and Child may have been less than perfect.

**Thomas and Ann Martin.** At the time of William Corder's trial in the summer of 1828, Ann Martin was 35 years old; her husband Thomas was 57.

*Above:* **Maria Martin's Cottage.** The cottage had five rooms and was occupied by Thomas Martin, his wife, three grown-up children, including Maria and her sister Ann, two adolescents, one child and one grandchild.

*Below:* **The Corder House.** Before John Corder died, he, his wife, three grown-up sons and one daughter and some servants occupied this substantial timber-framed house.

**The Red Barn**. Numerous illustrations of the Red Barn exist; this one, from the Bury Record Office, conforms generally to the outline of the barn and its accompanying buildings in the enclosure and tithe maps of the period, and shares many of the features of the picture published in Curtis's book as well as one printed in the *Sunday Times*. Following the enormous publicity surrounding the murder and trial, much of the outer cladding of the barn was stripped away by souvenir hunters. What was left burned down in 1842.

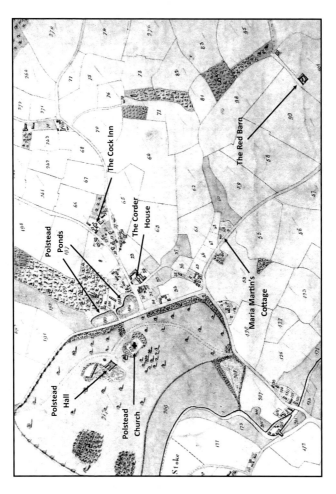

**Polstead** from the tithe map of 1833; key locations are identified.

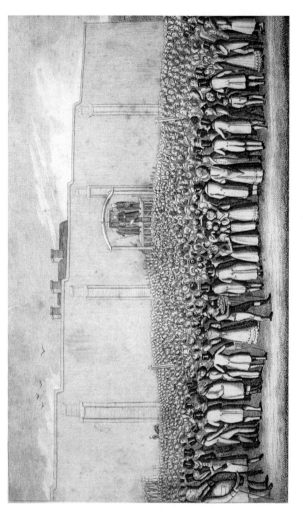

**The execution of William Corder.** According to Curtis, there were between eight and nine thousand spectators, 'including a great number of females ... some of rank and dressed in the first style of fashion'; the *Morning Chronicle* estimated 'upwards of 7,000' persons present.

as I did not see it when the body was first taken up in the Red Barn. The first time I saw the head was after the exhumation of the body. Mr Lawton showed it to me after the disinterment. I did not see it severed from the body, nor do I know, of my own knowledge, that it was that which was taken from the Red Barn. I took the heart from the body myself. A knife would have inflicted the wound I saw upon it.

Following a question from Mr Andrews:

I do not mean a knife of any size; but one which would correspond in breadth of blade with this sword. The wound was broader at that part of the ribs nearest the sternum – broader on one side than the other.

Since the identification of the head was called into question, possibly prompted by questions from Mr Brodrick, John Lawton was recalled to clarify when the head was removed and its subsequent history:

The head I showed to the last witness was the same I took from the body found in the Red Barn. I took it off when I assisted in removing the body from the barn. I then gave it to Baalham, the constable, who returned it to me ... a day or two after ... I am quite sure it was the same head which I showed to Mr Nairn.

John Baalham was recalled and confirmed that the same head that was taken from the body in the Red Barn was returned by him to Mr Lawton.

The prosecution now called a third medical man; he was Henry Robert Chaplin, who had also been present when Maria's body was exhumed. He was a surgeon of four years' experience. He examined the chest of the body, along with Mr Nairn. He confirmed the wounds on the heart; the one on the right ventricle appeared to have been recently inflicted. The second wound he was unable to say whether it was 'recently inflicted or an ancient wound'. He confirmed the existence of the wound between the ribs:

> I found a transverse wound situated between the fifth and sixth ribs, which appeared to have been inflicted with a weapon with a broad back and sharp edge. I did not see the sword fitted to the wound.

He went on to say that the wound in the heart appeared to be a continuation of the wound between the ribs, although he did not specify which wound in the heart, and confusingly, he said it could have resulted from the pericardium being stripped away. He thought the 'wound' to the heart would be fatal, although he would not swear to it. He had inspected the head, and found the appearance of a bullet wound – a wound which could not have been caused by decomposition – which might, or might not have been fatal. He also found a

> thrust in the eye, as if done by a sharp instrument with a broad back ... [which] might have been the same as inflicted that on the heart.

Finally, he could not say whether the bullet made its entry or exit wound from the eye. Following a question from the judge, he clarified that the thrust in the eye was the 'same eye as that which the ball had perforated', and that the weapon used might have been the same as that used in the ribs. There was a question from Mr Brodrick, following which Mr Chaplin said:

> If [the thrust in the eye] was done with such an instrument as I have seen [Corder's sword], it could not have perforated above the one-eighth of an inch. The instrument left an impression on the bone; it must have been a very sharp-pointed instrument.

As the judge examined the sword minutely, Mr Chaplin explained:

the sphenoidal sinus, or the sphenoidal bone, was the base of the cranium, or bottom of the skull.

In response to a question from Mr Brodrick regarding the heart wound(s):

A slight puncture in the heart might produce syncope, loss of blood, or fainting from the shock given to the system. I perceived no appearance of blood upon the heart

Then following a question from Mr Kelly on the gunshot wound to the head:

I think it not possible for any surgeon to say in what direction the bullet went, he might, if the bones had been broken away.

The judge, remembering Mr Lawton's evidence, asked:

Did this gentleman observe the bones of the nose, and how they got into the throat?

Mr Chaplin replied that he had not paid any attention to them.

Now Mr Lawton was recalled to demonstrate, using the sword together with Maria's skull, how the 'wound' on the sphenoidal sinus had occurred. Lawton went to the jury box, accompanied by Mr Brodrick, to show the jury what he thought had happened. The account by Curtis and that of *The Times* report are clearly incorrect. Other newspaper reports provide less detail, so exactly what Mr Lawton demonstrated is not very clear. Curtis (and *The Times*) stated that:

it appeared [to Mr Lawton] that the sword had entered by the sphenoidal sinus, traversed the mouth, hit the back part of the nose, and made its exit at the right eye.

The *Morning Chronicle* stated simply that 'the witness pointed out the direction where the bullet traversed and the sword pierced', and that 'the other way' the sword would not fit so well. *The Standard* report was similar. Curtis says next that Mr Lawton applied the sword

> to the supposed course of the instrument, which exactly agreed with the conjectural progress of the sword

But when he applied the sword to the other eye, 'it was found to be impossible to trace any opening from thence into the sphenoidal sinus'. Mr Lawton finished by commenting on the missing teeth in the skull. Again the press reports are contradictory; three teeth appeared to be missing, one from each side of the upper jaw, and one from the lower jaw. One had been drawn in life, another had decayed away. Yet another appeared to have fallen out since the body was originally discovered.

This was the last of the medical evidence for the prosecution. Since much of it was confused, and as shall be seen later, quite possibly incorrect in its conclusions, it is worthwhile trying to summarize what was said. Three medical men, all surgeons, gave evidence. Mr Lawton was present when the body was removed from the Red Barn. His initial findings on Maria's body, reported at the inquest, were that there was blood on the face and clothes, a pointed instrument appeared to have been thrust into the right eye and had displaced bones from the nose and orbit which he found in the throat; this thrust might have entered the brain and caused death, although the brain was too decomposed to yield any information. There was a shallow stab-wound in the neck and the handkerchief round the neck had been pulled unnaturally tight. He examined the heart, removing the pericardium – the membrane surrounding it – but detected no other wounds on the body. The head was removed for cleaning and analysis.

Subsequently, Mr Chaplin had a conversation with the mysterious Mr Glover, by which time Lawton had cleaned the head and now concluded that a bullet had entered the left jaw, and exited through the right eye. Mr Glover had supplied the information about the possible stab-wound in the ribs, having noticed a knife-shaped hole in the shift. Maria's body was exhumed, and Lawton being unable to be present, Messrs Nairn and Chaplin attended. A stab-wound was found between the fifth and sixth ribs, corresponding with the hole in the shift, and the heart was examined and found to have two 'wounds'. One, at the back of the right ventricle, Lawton admitted subsequently having made when he removed the pericardium from the heart; the second, near the apex of the heart, seemed to correspond with the thrust between the ribs. According to Nairn, the wound to the right ventricle was recent, the wound to the apex was not, although Chaplin said he could not judge. There was agreement, although Mr Chaplin was equivocal, that the gunshot wound to the head would probably not have been immediately fatal; Nairn said it might have been, although subsequently he said that it probably was not.

The evidence concerning the wound made in the sphenoidal sinus was confusing, and this is probably due to transcription errors by the press. The sword cannot have *entered* either via or by the sphenoidal sinus, which is one of two cavities situated deep inside the head, more or less behind the eye. It had suffered the wound or fissure made by the point of the instrument, and would have been at the end or bottom of the conjectured thrust.*

Presentation of the prosecution case now turned to the positive identification of the body found in the Red Barn as that of Maria Martin. Peter Mathews was recalled to prove that Maria had a 'small enlargement on the front of her neck,

---

* The evidence regarding the position of the sphenoidal sinus was also confusing; Nairn had said: 'the sphenoidal sinus, or base of the skull, corresponding with the situation of the vertebrae'. The sphenoidal sinuses, there are two of them, are small cavities in the skull; they lie well behind and between the eyes viewed from the front. If the 'base of the skull' is the position where it is joined to the vertebrae, then the sphenoidal sinuses are some distance above and forward of this point as a simple anatomical diagram will demonstrate.

which had the appearance of a wen'. Ann Martin was recalled and asked to identify the effects found on the body. These were produced by John Baalham. She identified the comb and earrings, two handkerchiefs, one silk, red and yellow, and one green, part of the leghorn hat trimmed with black 'riband', her shoes, an ashen busk (in her stays) and part of the chemise, all of which she said Maria was wearing the last time she saw her, when she went off with William Corder. At this point, Ann Martin was overcome, and Thomas Martin, Maria's father, was also seen to be shedding tears.

When she had composed herself, Mrs Martin was shown the black reticule bag which had been recovered from the house in Ealing during Corder's arrest. This she also identified, 'This is Maria's bag, I know it well'. The judge was not sure whether the bag constituted evidence, although Mr Andrews declared that it was important evidence, found as it was along with the sword. Ann Martin junior, Maria's sister, was now recalled, and she too identified both handkerchiefs, the shoes and the Leghorn bonnet as belonging to Maria; also the comb and earrings. Later, Maria's stepmother also confirmed that she was wearing white tape garters when she left with Corder. Mr Andrews stated that a passport for France, made out in Corder's name, was found in his desk, although the judge decided that that was doubtful evidence and should not be 'received'. Corder seemed grateful for this and bowed several time to the judge. Peter Mathews was then recalled again to confirm that Maria could write 'very well'; Thomas Martin confirmed that the soil in the Red Barn where the body was found was 'loose loam, stones and gravel, and very dry'.

That completed the evidence for the prosecution; Curtis noted that it had taken fourteen hours to present. The judge now called upon William Corder to present his defence. The prisoner took some handwritten notes from his pocket, adjusted his spectacles, and after bowing to the judge began in a 'tremulous' voice:

> My Lord, and Gentlemen of the jury, – I am informed
> that Counsel upon a trial, even where the life of a human
> being is involved, are not permitted, by the existing law
> of the country, to address the Jury on behalf of a prisoner,
> although on the part of the prosecution a contrary
> practice prevails.

After a plea to excuse any 'obscure or improperly arranged'
comments due to his anxiety of mind, he commented on the
difficulty of preparing a defence,

> as I have been, in entire ignorance of the evidence
> intended to be preferred against my life.

This was stretching the truth; Curtis called it 'altogether
a falsehood'. Corder had had the inquest evidence read to
him by his then solicitor, Mr Humphreys, although he was
unaware of the further submissions. Curtis commented that
'verbal communications had passed as enabled his solicitor to
anticipate the accusations.'

Corder went on to ask the jury to clear their minds of the
'disgusting details' on the case circulated by that 'powerful
engine' the press, where he had been described as 'the most
depraved of human monsters'. He then called their attention
to the conduct of his accusers; Mr Wayman, the coroner, had
subsequently instituted the prosecution:

> no man ought to act in first instance as judge, and
> afterwards as the professional accuser. The expectation
> that he is to act in the latter capacity, may influence his
> conduct in the former.

He went on:

> His Lordship, and you, gentlemen, will perceive that
> it probably did so in the present instance, – for at the
> inquest he refused to suffer me to be present whilst
> the witnesses were examined by him ... Such conduct

127

> ... appears to be most unjust ... because ... it is well known that the presence of the party whose conduct is under enquiry operates on the minds of the witnesses, and makes them more likely to adhere to a correct representation of what they really know.

These were very good points, and it is clear that even though the notes might have been in William Corder's handwriting, the content had been carefully considered by his counsel. He made further criticism of the coroner, 'either in his character as coroner, or as attorney for the prosecution', referring to the further depositions, taken largely on 3 June with a few on 25 May and some undated. Copies of these were refused to Corder, and even though the law allowed that refusal, the depositions ought, he said, to have been sworn before a magistrate, with Corder present. He continued:

> I have never until this day, heard any one of the witnesses against me examined ... Are witnesses to be privately and secretly examined on oath, and pinned down to a certain statement of circumstances behind the back of a prisoner? I am convinced, gentlemen, this can be neither just nor legal

After relating the misfortune of having lost three of his brothers within six months, and his father not long before, he addressed the charge against him: 'I have heard the indictment read, and the evidence offered to sustain it', and he admitted that the facts indicated 'the strongest suspicions of my guilt; but those facts are capable of explanation'. Then:

> I am well aware of my imprudence in having so long concealed the disclosures I am about to make, and that I have endangered my life by concealment; but I was stupefied and overwhelmed by the strange and disastrous occurrences from which guilt might so easily be inferred against the most innocent ... I acted

> with fear ... and having succeeded, in the first instance ... in concealing the death of Maria ... I ... persevered in falsehood, and have ... supplied evidence, which, unexplained, leads to the strong suspicion against me ... I am resolved to disclose the truth, regardless of the consequences.

William Corder now, at last, started to provide an explanation of what had happened:

> You have heard of the intimacy that subsisted between me and Maria, and of her pregnancy. In order to conceal from my mother and sister her situation, I provided lodgings for her at Sudbury ... where she was delivered of a male child. After the usual time, it was arranged that she should return to her father's with the infant, which she did, where she continued within doors, it not being known in the neighbourhood that she had come back. About a fortnight after her return, the child died in the arms of Mrs Marten, naturally, and not by violent means, as has been falsely given out by the newspapers ... it became necessary to bury the child; and as the birth ... had been concealed from my mother and family, and from the parish officers, it was agreed by Mrs Marten, Maria, and myself, that the child should be buried in the fields, though to Thomas Marten, Maria's father, it was represented that we were about to take it to Sudbury, where it was born, for interment. Accordingly, at night, Maria and I left her father's cottage with the child, and after burying it, I took her to my own home, where, there being a separate staircase, I was enabled to conduct her to my own bed-room, in which she was concealed the following day and night.

He described how he kept a pair of loaded pistols in his bedroom. He had shown Maria how to use them, and she knew that they had been repaired while they were in Sudbury. He said she must have taken them while she was there. He said Maria had been depressed for a long period, and pressed him to marry her. He was 'very much attached to her', but had declined to marry her, since his family disapproved of the connection, and she was still corresponding with Peter Mathews with 'whom she had had a child'. Maria persisted, however, 'alluding to [their] child', and she having produced in Corder a 'strong attachment', he agreed to marry her. In order to conceal the marriage from his mother, they decided to get married in Ipswich either by licence or banns. He said he could not remember whether he had said that there was a warrant out against Maria for having bastard children but:

> I was anxious that neither her return to Polstead nor her situation might be known to my mother or the neighbours; and it was for the same reason, I believe, that Maria dressed in male attire on the day in question

He said that Maria was crying bitterly when she left her father's house. Corder said that as they walked to the barn, he 'gently reproved her' for crying:

> it was not the way she should conduct herself to one who was willing to make every sacrifice to render her happy.

When they got to the barn, and while Maria was changing, she 'flew into a violent passion' and told Corder she cared nothing for him. He was too proud, she said, to take her to his mother's house. They would not be happy if they did marry, since Corder's mother and family 'would never notice her'. She upbraided Corder for not having as much regard for her as Peter Mathews. There was further 'conversation', and Corder said to Maria that

> if she would go on in this way before we were married, what could I expect afterwards

He said he had seen sufficient to convince him that he and Maria could never live happily together, and that he had resolved not to marry her and return home. He then left her, and had 'scarcely proceeded to the outer gate of the barn-yard', when he heard the report of a gun.* He ran back and found Maria on the ground, apparently dead. After some moments in 'complete stupefaction', and considering whether to run for help, he tried to raise Maria from the ground but found her lifeless. At this point in his account he made a very bad mistake. He said:

> I perceived the fatal weapon, which I took up, when, to add to my terror, and the extraordinary singularity of my situation, I discovered it to be one of my own pistols, *which I had always kept loaded in my bed-room.* [Author's italics]

Ann Martin, Maria's stepmother, had stated in her evidence that Corder had had a gun in his hand, when he went away with Maria:

> I believe the gun was loaded, because he told me so. I said "Is it charged?" and he said, "Yes, don't let the child (alluding to the little boy) meddle with it"

Curtis pointed out this anomaly, also commenting that 'from good authority', Corder was in the habit of carrying his pistols with him in his 'ordinary walks'.

William Corder continued with his statement. He realized, he said, how suspicious the circumstances would be were he to have reported what had happened, and decided to bury Maria in the barn. He went on:

> if I were innocent, why should I do all this? I answer that observation by stating, that a man may, through fear,

---

*    Curtis claimed that at one point, the defence offered was to be that Maria threatened William with the pistol she had stolen from him unless he 'took her to Ipswich and married her'; there was a struggle, he managed to get the pistol from her, but it went off by accident.

pursue the same conduct that another man may from guilt; and, situated as I was, I ask whether it might not have occurred to you or any other man to act as I did.

He pointed out that it was impossible to prove this statement since there were no witnesses, and reiterated that Maria must have stolen the pistols from his bedroom – he found the second pistol in her bag – and he claimed that he had not missed them as he had 'no occasion to use the pistols'.

He now came to one of the mysteries associated with the Red Barn murder:

It has, I believe, been reported by some of the witnesses, that the body had the appearance of having been stabbed and contused. All I can say in answer to this, is that no stab or wound was ever inflicted by me; and I believe the surgeons would never have thought of stabs or wounds, had it not been that a small sword was found in my possession

Curtis said that Corder was frequently heard to say to a fellow prisoner: 'That sword will hang me!' Corder went on to comment on the difficulty of being able to 'speak satisfactorily on the subject' (of the stab wounds) since the body was in an advanced state of decomposition. He said he could only account for the wounds by supposing that they had been made accidentally when the body was being searched for and subsequently disinterred.

He now came to the question of motive. Regarding the intended marriage, his friends disapproved of it and there were Maria's 'irregularities with another individual'. He implied that he could easily have broken it off. He pointed out that they went to the barn in the middle of the day, 'in the neighbourhood of cottages' and in the full knowledge of Maria's family. If he had intended to commit the crime, he should have chosen a 'very different time, place and opportunity'. He said that he had not fled the crime scene, staying in Polstead for at least four months until he was sent to a watering place for his health. He commented on the passport for France for himself and his wife found in his possession; it was obtained in order to visit a friend of his wife's in Paris, but he declined to go on account of the expense, pointing out that he could, at any time, have fled if he were guilty. There was the question of some of Maria's things found in his possession:

> is it possible to believe that I should have preserved them had I been conscious of my guilt?

He then asked the jury whether publishing his name and address in *The Times* advertising for sale the lease of his wife's house was the action of a man seeking to conceal himself. He finished by conceding that his accusers were 'justified, from the circumstances ... in submitting the case for judgement'. His fault was, he said, in concealing the circumstances. His conscience told him that he was 'fairly and honestly entitled' to an acquittal. He finished: 'my life is in your hands'.

William Corder's statement had taken thirty-two minutes to read, during which time, according to Curtis, 'there was the most profound silence in court'. The pronunciation of some words, Curtis says, indicated that he was not a man of education. The statement was in his own handwriting, and had been altered several times, notably, in reference to Peter Mathews and the missing five-pound note. However, some very good legal points were made, and some of Corder's more inexplicably stupid actions, notably the publication of his name and address in *The Times*, were presented as proof of his innocence.

Witnesses for the defence were now heard, although these amounted to little more than to character. William and Mary Ann Goodwin of Plough Lane, Sudbury had provided Maria with lodgings during her confinement with Corder's child. William Goodwin said that Corder visited two or three times a week and 'I never saw anything to induce me to think they were not fond of one another'. Maria had told him that she had gone to see 'Mr Harcourt, the gun-smith, about some pistols', although the judge said that was 'no evidence at all'. His wife confirmed that Maria had been alone to the gunsmith's about the pistols. She added that Maria and William 'appeared to be much attached to each other', although Maria was frequently in poor spirits.

Thomas Hardy was employed on the Corder farm. He remembered seeing William Corder with Maria on 13 May 1827 walking across the yard (at the Corders' house) at around nine in the evening. He confirmed that there were two staircases and that Corder could get to his room without his mother's knowledge. He also stated that he had seen Corder cleaning his pistols around that time.

Lucy Baalham had been in service with William's mother for eleven months, 'until last Old Michaelmas Day'.* She confirmed that William stayed with his mother until around two weeks before she (Lucy) left. She said that she had seen Corder's pistols in his bedroom, 'sometimes ... in and sometimes outside of the box'. As to his character:

> He always behaved like a kind and good-natured young man.

Edward Living was a surgeon from Nayland. He had attended Corder professionally, and around August of 1827 had advised him to leave Polstead and

> go to a warm bathing place ... Hastings, or some other place on the south coast ... he exhibited strong symptoms of consumption ... I recommended him to

---

* Michaelmas Day is 29 September; 'Old' Michaelmas Day, according to the 'Old Style' Julian calendar, would have been 11 days later following the adoption of the Gregorian calendar in 1752. In 1827 it would have fallen on 10 October.

remove, thinking that the change might be beneficial to his health.

Theresa Havers said that she had known Corder from his infancy, and always thought him a 'kind, good-tempered, and humane man'. John Bugg was a 'looker-on' on one of Mrs Corder's farms. He had known Corder since he was a baby, and he always appeared to be kind and humane. John Pryke was at school with Corder:

> I have known William Corder intimately from a child; we were school-fellows together. I have never heard any thing since to the contrary that he was a kind, humane young man. I believe him to have been such.

Mary Kersey was a cousin by marriage to William Corder, and lived in Bury St Edmunds. She said that he was a kind, good-tempered young man. Jeremiah Borham, William's brother-in-law, married to his eldest sister Mary, deposed:

> I am a miller, and live at Sproughton. I have known Corder from his childhood. I never knew any thing of him but being a kind young man – that's his character.

William Baalham, the 20-year-old son of John Baalham, the village constable, had known Corder for several years: 'He used to appear to me to be a kind, humane, good-tempered young man.'

That completed the case for the defence. It is appropriate, at this point, to make a few comments on it. Corder started his defence statement by mentioning that his counsel, Mr Brodrick, was not allowed to address the jury on his behalf. That was indeed the law at the time, although it was changed in 1836 by the Prisoners' Counsel Act, which also gave the prisoner the right to a copy of the depositions against him – including those made post committal. Corder pointed out that the depositions in the inquest were not made in his presence, and neither he nor his counsel received copies of the evidence taken subsequently. He questioned how Mr Wayman, the coroner, could act without prejudice in the capacity of both judge (at the inquest) and prosecutor (at the assize hearing). Corder also raised the question of the highly prejudicial pre-trial publicity. The law on this point was quite clear:

> stirring up prejudice against an accused awaiting trial was prohibited on pain of committal for contempt. But it was a prohibition to which the press paid little heed[9]

Just a month later at the Old Bailey, Justice (Sir Stephen) Gazelee, summing up in a forgery case, commented:

> It is much to be lamented that in the present day no case of any importance now occurs in which public opinion is not forestalled by the accounts which somehow or other find their way into the newspapers, and which create a prejudice against the accused parties, from which it is very difficult, if not impossible, for juries to divest themselves[10]

It is notable that the witnesses who spoke to William Corder's character used the same words again and again to describe him: 'kind', 'humane' and 'good-tempered'. It might be suspected that a little coaching had taken place, with Mr Brodrick helping them with what to say. There can be no suspicion though of corruption; the witnesses were under oath and were God-fearing people. It is highly unlikely that they stated facts which they knew to be untrue. William Corder, on the other hand, did not speak under oath, which was the law at the time.

It is also notable that William made what was probably a fatal error in claiming that Maria stole his pistols when she stayed in his room, saying that he always kept them there, when her stepmother, sister and stepbrother had given evidence on the first day of the trial to the effect that he had at least one loaded gun with him when he left with Maria to go to the Red Barn. Mr Brodrick, Corder's defence counsel, for all of his 140 guineas fee and an assistant, had failed to identify this enormous flaw in William's statement which they would have had plenty of time to rectify had they spotted it.

The judge did not fail to spot it, however. He began his summing-up 'a little before twelve o'clock' and spoke for two hours. He started by reminding the jury that they had to decide whether William Corder had caused the death of Maria Martin by one of the several ways in the indictment, or by a combination of them: shooting, stabbing, strangling and suffocation by burying alive. Before getting into the detail though, he reiterated something that the prisoner had 'very properly said' regarding the

> prejudices which have been raised against him, not only in the county of Suffolk, but throughout the kingdom generally. It is very unfortunate ... extremely so ... inasmuch as they often place the life of the prisoner in more jeopardy ... It appears that accounts of this transaction have found their way into the newspapers ... I am free to say that such publications are certainly mischievous and injurious to him ... We have heard that placards have been dispersed, not only in the neighbourhood where the transaction took place, not only in the neighbourhood of this town, but in the vicinity of this very hall, tending to the manifest detriment of the prisoner at the bar. Such a practice is so ungenerous and unjust, that I cannot bring myself to give credence that any person, even of the very lowest class of society, can so far degrade himself as to attempt a derivation of gain from the exhibition of this melancholy transaction.

It might be wondered, given that even the newspapers were practising what was, in effect, contempt of court, that nothing was done. These remarks of Lord Chief Baron Alexander in a murder trial, coupled with those, already reported, of Justice

Gazelee in a forgery case – which attracted the death penalty – and made only a few weeks later, ought to have stimulated some action, but none was taken. However it was not only the newspapers and 'street entertainers' that could prejudice the trial:

> it is the assertion, that a minister of the gospel quitted the place where he normally performed divine service, and erected his pulpit very near the scene of this melancholy tragedy; and there endeavoured to inflame the passions and excite the resentment of the populace against the prisoner ... I cannot conceive any act which is more contrary to the spirit and principles of the religion of which he professes himself to be a minister

Curtis had reported this event. On 22 of June 1828, 'Reverend' Mr Young, from London, had preached a sermon 'in a large open space, a short distance from, and in view of, the Red Barn'. Handbills advertising the event had been printed, and Curtis reported that the village green opposite the Cock Inn was crowded with carriages and chaises. Up to five thousand people had come to listen to Mr Young, who took his address from Ezekiel, chapter xxxiii, verse 11:

> As I live, saith the Lord God, I have no pleasure in the death of the wicked; but that the wicked turn from his way and live: turn ye turn ye from your evil ways; for why will ye die, O house of Israel?

It is not clear whether 'the wicked' referred to was the murderer, whom Curtis insisted was not named, but who was likely to die, or Maria, the unfortunate victim, who had sinned in the flesh and who had died. According to Curtis, the judge was mistaken; the preacher had not 'excited the resentment of the populace against the prisoner'. Curtis also commented on the camera obscura that Mr Brodrick referred to when he was cross-examining Mr Chaplin. He said that it exhibited a picture of the Red Barn which, 'by the aid of a powerful magnifying glass' appeared twenty times larger than the original print. The placard attached to 'this caravan' simply stated that a likeness of William Corder could be obtained for the price of sixpence, at a shop near the Abbey Gate in Bury.

The judge, after having reminded the jury of their duties towards the prisoner, commented that a 'very considerable part of the [prosecution] evidence', that relating to establishing the identity of the body found in the Red Barn, was rendered unnecessary, since the prisoner in his defence had declared that the body was that of Maria Martin. He called their attention to the fact that the prisoner had 'seduce[d] her from home' by the fiction that there was a warrant out against Maria for her bastard children. Maria had been in low spirits on the day she left for the Red Barn and had been so 'for some time past'. Crucially, he reminded them that Mrs Martin had sworn that the prisoner 'snapped his pistols' by the fireside before he went to the Red Barn – proving that they were in his possession at the time and not Maria's.

He called their attention to the evidence of Maria's father that he put his mole-spike 'into [the body] about the hip', and that the 'smallest end of the spike was thicker than the thinnest part of his little finger'.* He reminded them that Lea, the police officer, confirmed that the depositions from the inquest were read over to the prisoner, commenting that that '[takes] away the sting of the accusation that had been made against Mr Wayman'. He questioned why, if the prisoner's statement that Maria had committed suicide was true, he did not mention it to Lea when arrested, repeatedly insisting that he never knew 'any such person' as Maria Martin.

The judge now came to the medical evidence. Mr Lawton, the surgeon, had confirmed the wound to the head by the pistol

---

* The implication being that the 'stab' wounds on Maria's body would be unlikely to have been caused by the mole-spike.

ball, but also the wounds in the 'neck, heart and ribs ... inflicted with a sharp instrument', as well as possible strangulation with a handkerchief. He asked the jury to consider whether Maria committed suicide by shooting herself and stabbing herself several times, and what credence, therefore, to give to the medical evidence in the light of the story told by the prisoner as to what had happened. He reminded them that the prisoner told them that he and Maria had had a violent and passionate dispute, following which he left her in the barn, returning when he heard the shot. He admitted burying Maria in the Red Barn, and making various untrue statements regarding her whereabouts afterwards. He told the jury that they had to decide upon the 'truth or falsehood of [Corder's] representations today', adding that the evidence for the defence had shown him to have a 'mild temper and humane character':

> Upon this, gentlemen, I have only one remark to make; and that is, that character, however good it may have been, can be of no avail where it comes in opposition to direct and conclusive evidence – it is only where the balance is equal that the evidence of character can lend its preponderating influence

The judge addressed the complaint made by Corder in his defence statement against the coroner/prosecutor Mr Wayman. There was no right for parties implicated by evidence in an inquest to be present, although it was usual to allow it. However, Lea's testimony confirmed that the evidence was read over to the prisoner afterwards, so the prisoner had 'no right either to complain or to cast ungenerous speculations on others'.

Coming back to the evidence, the judge again told the jury that they had to decide whether the prisoner's defence statement was true or false. He reminded them again about the possession of the pistols, and that the prisoner had not cross-examined either Maria's stepmother or sister on the point. He then came to the question of the alleged suicide:

> We all know that it is a circumstance which too often happens, that poor girls, when they have been disappointed in their expectations, have laid rash hands upon themselves ... generally ... strangulation or poison. In this case, if you give credit to the evidence of the surgeons ... There were, first, the wounds in the eye and cheek, inflicted by a ball; and then the wounds inflicted with a sharp instrument, that was broader on one side than the other, on the heart and ribs; and ... on the vertebrae of the neck behind the skull[*]

He went on:

> It is a very extraordinary thing, that instead of hanging herself on a tree, as poor infatuated and disappointed girls generally do ... Maria Marten should have used two different means to kill herself

The judge repeated that the jury must decide on the credibility of the medical evidence, and the possibility that all the wounds could have been caused by Maria herself. He told them that if they had the least doubt, the prisoner should have the benefit of it. But:

> should you be thoroughly satisfied that the representations made by him are false ... it will be your duty to serve your country manfully and fearlessly ... and discharge with fidelity the solemn oath which you have sworn, by returning a verdict of guilty

The foreman of the jury requested that they be allowed to retire to deliberate which they did at ten minutes to two in the afternoon. They returned 35 minutes later. The clerk of the

---

[*] By vertebrae he was referring to the sphenoidal sinus which one of the surgeons had commented was adjacent to the vertebrae.

court asked them if they were agreed in their verdict; they said that they were, unanimously.

Clerk of the court:

> How say you gentlemen, is the prisoner at the bar, William Corder, guilty of the murder of which he stands indicted, or not guilty?

Foreman, in a 'faltering' voice,

> Guilty!

Clerk of the court:

> Hearken to your verdict, gentlemen. You say that William Corder, the prisoner, is Guilty, and so say you all?

Foreman:

> Yes, we do.

And knowing the inevitable sentence that was about to be passed upon him, William Corder had to listen to an unseemly row that had broken out between James Lea the policeman and Mr Orridge the prison governor regarding ownership of Corder's pistols – which Corder had promised to Lea. Silence was demanded as the judge donned the black coif and addressed the prisoner:

> William Corder, it now becomes my most painful duty to announce to you the near approach of your mortal career. You have been accused of Murder, which is the highest offence that can be found in the annals of crime. You denied your guilt, and put yourself upon your deliverance to your country ... a jury of that country has decided against you, and that decision is most just.

He then proceeded to lecture Corder on 'thou shalt not kill', and 'he that sheddeth man's blood, by man shall his blood be shed'. He had not the slightest hope of mercy on earth, but having sent 'this unfortunate woman to her account, with all her imperfections on her head', he would be allowed a 'small interval' for preparation:

> listen to the voice of the ministers of religion who will, I trust, advise and console you, so that you may be able to meet with becoming resignation and fortitude that dreadful ordeal which you will have shortly to undergo.

The judge then pronounced the sentence of death:

> That you be taken back to the prison from whence you came, and that you be taken from thence, on Monday next, to a place of execution, and that you be there hanged by the neck until you are dead; and that your body afterwards be dissected and anatomized; and may the Lord God Almighty, of his infinite goodness, have mercy on your soul!

William Corder was supported by Mr Orridge and one of his assistants, and was taken sobbing from the bar; one of the lady witnesses for the defence fainted in court.

# The Final Act

It was Friday afternoon, and William Corder had the rest of that day as well as Saturday and Sunday to prepare himself for what was to happen at midday on Monday. He was taken from the court to prison by a chaise on to which swarmed the public in an attempt to see him, breaking the steps of the chaise. Once in the prison he was obliged to change into prison attire, grey frieze with yellow and black stripes, and placed in the condemned cell accompanied by two warders to prevent the possibility of suicide.

His wife, accompanied by her companion Mrs Atherton, visited William on Saturday afternoon and stayed for about half an hour; she left him with a copy of *The Companion to the Altar*, which according to Curtis he read 'with profound attention'. He attended the prison chapel, where the chaplain, Revd Mr Stocking, read a 'discourse on the last judgement' to him. He was visited later by Revd Mr Sheen, who was the chaplain to the High Sheriff.

On Sunday he attended service in the prison chapel conducted by Revd Stocking. The press were admitted, and Corder was reported to be holding a white handkerchief to his face the entire time. Curtis provided a commentary regarding the service, the sermon and Corder's occasional reactions to them, apparently relishing the gruesome detail. Corder was conducted back to his cell after the service and 'sobbed on his bed for many minutes'. His wife then visited him for the last time. According to Curtis, William advised her not to marry again, or if she did, not to marry anyone in response to an advertisement. He was visited again by Revd Stocking who advised him that 'He that confesseth and forsaketh his sins, should find mercy'. At around nine o'clock in the evening, Mr Orridge sent him a paper, apparently written by him, on the subject of confession:

Confession to the world has always been held a necessary atonement where the party has committed offences affecting the interests of society at large ... The Christian doctrine of the necessity of restitution is strong, and if you do not confess, how can you make restitution to the reputation of your victim? You have accused her of murdering herself. If you die without denying that accusation, how do you obey the command, 'to do that to another, which we would have another do to us?'

After a comment that the duty of 'acknowledgement of public crime' had nothing to do with Popish confession, the governor signed the note 'John Orridge'. Orridge visited William after he had read the note, and wrote the following to William's dictation:

Bury Gaol, Aug 10, 1828, Condemned Cell, Sunday evening, half-past 11.

I acknowledge being guilty of the death of poor Maria Marten, by shooting her with a pistol. The particulars are as follows:– When we left her father's house we began quarrelling about the burial of the child, she apprehending that the place wherein it was deposited would be found out. The quarrel continued for about three-quarters of an hour, upon this and other subjects. A scuffle ensued, and during the scuffle, and at the time I think she had hold of me, I took the pistol from the side-pocket of my velveteen jacket, and fired. She fell, and died in an instant. I never saw even a struggle. I was overwhelmed with agitation and dismay – the body fell near the front doors on the floor of the barn. A vast quantity of blood issued from the wound, and ran on to the floor and through the crevices. Having determined to bury the body in the barn (about two hours after she was dead) I went and borrowed the spade of Mrs Stow; but before I went there, I dragged the body from the barn into the chaff-house, and locked up the barn. I returned again to the barn and began to dig the hole; but the spade being a bad one, and the earth firm and hard, I was obliged to go home for a pickaxe and a better spade, with which I dug the hole, and then buried the body. I think I dragged the body by the handkerchief that was tied round her neck – it was dark when I finished covering up the body. I went the next day, and washed the blood from off the barn floor. I declare to Almighty God I had no sharp instrument about me, and that no other wound but the one made by the pistol was inflicted by me. I have been guilty of great idleness, and at times led a dissolute life, but I hope through the mercy of God to be forgiven.

W Corder

Witness to the signing by the said William Corder, John Orridge, Sunday Evening, half-past 12 o'clock.

Having had the night to think about it, the confession was read to him again just before his execution:

Condemned Cell, 12 o'clock Monday Morning, Aug 11, 1828

The above confession was read over carefully to the prisoner in our presence, who stated most solemnly that it was true; and that he had nothing to add or to retract from it.

W Stocking, Chaplain

Timothy R Holmes, Under-Sherrif

Curtis added two other things: Corder acknowledged the fraud on the bank for the ninety-three pounds, which his wife had subsequently repaid, and he denied again, in the presence of Dr Probert and the undersheriff, that he had a sharp instrument with him on the day of the murder. He did, however, opine that the pistol ball which killed Maria had entered the right eye.[*]

On Monday, people started arriving at Bury at five o'clock in the morning. The execution was to take place in a paddock outside the prison walls. Normally, condemned prisoners would be escorted through the prison front door, into the high road, and then into the paddock on the north-east side of the gaol, the scaffold being erected in the middle of the paddock. For William Corder's execution, the anticipated crowd would probably have made it impossible to conduct the proceedings in an orderly manner. Accordingly, an opening was made in the north-east wall of the prison, and a special door was fitted into it, the scaffold being erected close to the door. It was called 'Corder's door'; according to Curtis, one of the workmen nicknamed it 'Corder's Passage to Eternity'.

Corder was visited by the chaplain in his cell, and then at nine-thirty he attended a service in the chapel where he partook of the Holy Sacrament. He was dressed in his own clothes, the same clothes he wore for the trial. He wrote to his wife, and after hoping that heaven would bless her and protect her, he said that, within the hour, he would be in heaven and:

> The awful sentence which has been passed upon me, and which I am now summoned to answer, I confess is very just

At half-past eleven, Corder was taken from his cell and had his arms pinioned and his wrists tied together at the front. The effect was as though he was at prayer, and this was the custom with those about to be executed, presumably to allow

---

[*] According to the surgeons, the pistol ball made its exit at the right eye.

them to pray until the very last moment. Then, according to Curtis who said it was Corder's last wish, he was taken round to the different 'wards' of the prison to say goodbye and shake hands with many of the prison inmates, some of whom he had known since childhood. Curtis noted that the prison governor, Mr Orridge, thought this action was calculated 'to prove beneficial to the juvenile offenders in particular'. Corder was then conducted through the specially-made door and on to the scaffold, in procession with the undersheriff, the prison governor, Mr Stocking the chaplain and various prison guards. There was a 'momentary buzz in the crowd,' which Curtis estimated to be between eight and nine thousand strong, and all the men took off their hats. When all was ready, Mr Orridge asked Corder if he had any last words. He said:

> I am guilty – my sentence is just – I deserve my fate – and may God have mercy on me!

Orridge then announced in a loud voice to the assembled throng:

> The prisoner acknowledges his sentence to be just, and declares that he dies in peace with all mankind.

To which several responded: 'Does he? Then may the Lord have mercy on his soul'. So far, so good, but then the executioner, John Foxton, nearly botched the whole process.* He was the Newgate hangman, brought specially to Suffolk for this notable event – there had not been a public execution in Bury for three years. But Foxton was getting on. He had been doing the job for forty years and was known to enjoy a drink; he would be dead himself the following year. Five years previously, his intended victim at Ipswich having been reprieved at the last moment,

---

\* His name may have been 'Foxon'. Curtis and several newspapers called him 'Foxton', but a report in *The Standard* of 27 December 1828 of an execution at Chelmsford, named him 'Foxon'.

he had drunk himself into such a state that the London coach refused to allow him on board.[1]

The black hood had been drawn over Corder's head, but Foxton seemed to be having trouble with his knots:

> [He] kept the victim in a suspense of at least five minutes, by the awkward manner in which he had adjusted the rope. He attempted to knot it several times; and at one period after having tied it, as he thought, at a sufficient length, he was obliged to unloose it, and contract the fall in which it would give.[2]

It was customary to have a 'drop' of less than three feet, and one report suggested that comments were made to the effect that the rope was too long. Curtis said that Foxton 'did not relish this interference with his public functions'. He then descended from the scaffold, and evidently still annoyed at the meddling with his professional activities and aware of the prison governor's displeasure with the delay, he 'severed with a knife, the rope that supported the platform' before the chaplain had said his final prayer and the signal had been given. Foxton then grasped the prisoner around the waist to add his weight to that of the prisoner's; the victim's neck was not broken by the short drop and death resulted from strangulation. The hangman at least ensured that the agony was over as soon as possible. Curtis noted that Corder was in a state of near fainting at the end, and could not, in any case, have stood for more than another minute; the prison governor, he said, did not regret Foxton's premature action. Foxton was reported as saying later:

> I never like to be meddled with, because I always study the subjects which come under my hands, and, according as they are tall or short, heavy or light, I accommodate them with the fall. No man in England has had so much experience as me, or knows how to do his duty better.[3]

After an hour, the body was cut down and removed to the Shire Hall for the inspection of the public. Thus ended the mortal career of William Corder, but in death, as in the latter part of his life, he remained a subject of enormous public interest. The clothes were removed from the top part of his body, and the county surgeon, Mr Creed, opened the chest to expose the muscles. The public were then admitted to view the remains, which many thousands did, of both sexes, 'some of high respectability'. Then the head was shaved and plaster casts were made, after which the body was removed to the county hospital for dissection in front of a large number of medical men and students.

Before the body was taken for dissection, Foxton claimed the trousers and stockings to which, apparently, he had a right. Perhaps he sold them to someone looking for a bizarre souvenir. More bizarre though was the fate of the rope; there had been a scuffle among the spectators as people sought to obtain parts of it after the body was cut down. The newspapers reported that it sold for a guinea an inch; Foxton commented later:

> What I got, I got, and that's all I shall say, except that that are [sic] was a very good rope.[4]

It has been said that the treatment of Corder's body was cruel, and it was unnecessary for the judge to have ordered dissection. In fact, he had no choice; the Murder Act of 1751, declared that: 'in no case whatsoever the body of any murderer shall be suffered to be buried'. The requirement was that the body be dissected and anatomized or, alternatively, hung in chains on a gibbet. The act did, however, appear to allow what was left, if anything, to be buried afterwards. Lord Lansdowne's Offences Against the Person Act, 1828, which came into effect on 1 July 1828, just before William Corder's trial, repealed the Murder Act, but in respect of what happened to the bodies of executed murderers it was unchanged; section 4 stated:

the body of every murderer shall, after execution, either
be dissected or hung in chains, as the court shall seem
meet

Thus Lord Chief Baron Alexander had little discretion in the
matter; he opted for dissection and anatomization, which must
have been slightly less awful for everyone concerned than
hanging the body publicly in chains.

# *Aftermath*

William Corder had been hanged on Monday 11 August 1828.[1] The daily newspapers had full accounts of the proceedings, as did the Sunday newspapers of the following weekend, and various aspects of the story dragged on until September. But it was the *Sunday Times* that ran the most newsworthy story. This related to Corder's final confession, made less than twelve hours before his execution. The three surgeons who variously examined Maria Martin's body, both immediately after it was discovered, and a month later when it was exhumed, stated that as well as a gunshot to the head, she had suffered various stab wounds. These included a stab to the eye – evidence for which was a puncture mark in the bone of the sphenoidal sinus – a stab to the neck and a stab to the heart between the fifth and sixth ribs. The medical men were of course country surgeons, not forensic pathologists, but they had plenty of experience between them so their opinions had to count for something.

Nevertheless, Corder always denied stabbing Maria, even in his final confession when he admitted shooting her with his pistol. One explanation offered for this apparent anomaly, made among others by Corder himself in his defence statement, was that the stab wounds found on the body had been made accidentally by Thomas Martin's mole-spike during his search of the Red Barn. He was probing the ground and at one point the spike came up with something adhering to it that 'smelt ... disagreeable'. He said in his evidence that he thought the spike had penetrated the body near the thigh, although none of the surgeons reported such a wound. An 'eminent and respectable physician', not named, claimed that the wounds could have been made by the spade or 'spud' at the other end of the mole-spike. He said that the thrust to the heart had not 'injured the major cavities' and would not have caused the 'effusion of blood'. He also commented that the wound to the throat was longitudinal (presumably vertical is meant), rather than transverse which would have been more likely if the throat was cut.[2] But the *Sunday Times* of 17 August ran the following headline:

Corder's Confession True – The Surgeons' Accounts of the Stabs Mistaken

Followed by:

The declaration of Corder in almost the hour of death, when no possible motive could exist for misrepresentation or concealment, first led to the opinion that the surgeons might have been unintentionally mistaken, and this opinion was subsequently strengthened by what passed in the dissecting room of the hospital [there had been a heated discussion regarding Maria's stab wounds]. Mr Orridge exerted himself to ascertain the truth of the several rumours that were in circulation, and has most satisfactorily been enabled to determine that the stabs were not, as is supposed, inflicted by Corder, but that the wounds that appeared on the apex of the heart and between the 5th and 6th ribs, were the consequence of what perhaps may be termed the conscientious curiosity of one of the jurymen on the coroner's inquest, who, anxious to discover how far decomposition had advanced, plunged a knife into the body between the ribs ... This fact, which can be incontrovertibly established, satisfactorily accounts for the presence of the wounds, and contradicts the supposition that they were caused ... by the mole-spike

Then:

> By this discovery, two things are clearly demonstrated;
> the one, that Corder's confession ... may be depended on
> ... and ... the professional [medical] gentlemen ... were
> in error.[3]

This was an astonishing revelation, but was it true? Orridge, made no direct mention of it in a subsequent letter to Curtis although a careful reading suggests that he may well have been involved; Curtis never mentioned it at all. Did the *Sunday Times* reporter get it wrong and embellish a mere rumour that was circulating? But if that had been the case, for such an important development which named the prison governor as having conducted the investigation, surely a denial at least would have been issued? None was, and there were further reports about the claim. A few days later, the *Bury and Norwich Post* related details of the dissection of Corder's body:

> Considerable discussion arose amongst the medical
> gentlemen as to ... Corder's declaration that no stabs
> were inflicted by him ... It seemed to be the opinion of
> some ... that the wounds might have been inflicted by
> the mole-spike ... *Something, however, has been said
> about one of the villagers having thrust his knife through
> the "case of the ribs" when the body was found, but the
> statement cannot be traced to its author* [author's italics][4]

The *Bury and Suffolk Herald*, on the same day quoted the piece from the *Sunday Times* at length saying that 'it was going the round of the London newspapers', but denied that Orridge was involved. The (*Sunday Times*) story, it said, wanted the 'corroboration of a living witness to attest to the "fact"'.[5]

In the same edition, the *Bury and Suffolk Herald* published a letter from one of the surgeons, John Charles Nairn, who was responding to questions raised about the veracity of their findings in the light of Corder's denial of any stabbing. He said that the gunshot wound alone could not have killed Maria, and also questioned Corder's statement about the heavy bleeding, given the path of the bullet. He said that these conclusions were not just his but that he had consulted 'several respectable members of the profession'. He cited a gruesome incident at Waterloo where a soldier had half of his face shot off with very little bleeding. He went on to 'prove' how the mole-*spade* could not have made the wounds in the body when Thomas Martin was probing the ground looking for the body, but failed to mention the possibility that the mole-*spike* could have done it.[*]

Two weeks later, Nairn had another letter published responding to the story about the enthusiastic juryman.[6] He had been assured, he said, that none of the jurymen touched the body; he didn't say who had assured him. On the question of the thrust in the ribs and the corresponding wound in the heart he commented on:

> the moral impossibility for a knife to cause the two wounds at one and the same time, in consequence of the collapsed state in which the viscera were, unless its blade had been at least nine or ten inches in length[†]

But the viscera were 'collapsed' because Lawton had opened the chest on 20 April during the first session of the inquest and removed the tissue surrounding the heart. Nairn himself, in his evidence during the trial, commented on the 'good state of preservation' of the internal parts of the chest. If a juryman made the wound, he must have made it before Lawton removed the shift and opened the chest, otherwise the shift would not have had a hole in it. If that were the case, then the wound was

---

[*] Thomas Martin's mole-spade had a narrow spade or 'spud' at one end for digging, and an iron spike at the other for making a hole in the ground in which to put a springy twig that was part of the mole trap.

[†] The point being made was that if the viscera were 'collapsed', the heart would have been a long way from the wound in the ribs and the 'enthusiastic juryman' would have needed a very long knife.

made when the viscera were still intact, either when Maria was killed, or during the disinterment and examination of the body. Regarding the wound in the neck, Nairn said:

> as soon as the handkerchiefs had been removed from the face and neck ... one of the first things that attracted our attention, was the wound beneath them; this could not have been previously made by the mole-spade, otherwise there would have been a corresponding cut in the handkerchiefs, which *I* can vouch was not the case, neither could it have been inflicted by the "conscientious" juryman, for Mr Lawton untied, and removed the handkerchief *himself*.

But of course, Nairn wasn't there; Lawton was the only surgeon present on 20 April. In his evidence to the inquest, he said:

> The handkerchief had apparently been pulled tight about the neck and there was a space between the outer fold of it and the tight part sufficient for a hand to have been inserted. In the neck just below the fold of the handkerchief there was the appearance of a wound inflicted by some sharp instrument but the part was in such a state of decomposition that I can only state it had that appearance.

The words 'just below the fold', imply that the wound was not beneath, i.e., covered by the fold, but below it, further down the neck, since if the handkerchief had been removed, it would have been difficult to have referenced the wound to the fold. If that was the case, then Nairn's suggestion was wrong, and the wound *could* have been caused by the juryman without making a hole in either handkerchief. In fact Lawton had said in his statement in court: 'I removed the handkerchief *principally* myself [author's italics]'. He also said: 'I assisted in taking off the clothes' which implies that at least one other person was involved. Perhaps that person was the enthusiastic juryman with a knife...

Of course, Lawton failed to notice the thrust between the ribs, and then removed the head in order to investigate fully the track of the bullet. It was, therefore, impossible to ascertain anything more about the wound in the neck or the possible marks of strangulation. Nairn found the stab wound in the side when the body was exhumed a month later, but then he was looking for it, the mysterious Mr Glover having told him about the hole in the shift. Glover had found the hole during the 'nauseating investigation of bloody folds' in the shift.[7] That of itself is interesting. If Maria had been stabbed by Corder and bled into her shift, then after eleven months in the ground that blood would have dried; Glover talking about 'nauseating ... bloody folds', suggests that the 'blood' might still have been moist. If that were the case, the so-called blood would be much more likely to have been recently-released putrefying bodily fluids, perhaps resulting from a stab wound made at the time of the inquest.

When Lawton was first examining the 'chest and abdomen' looking for wounds, as well as missing a three-quarter to one inch wide stab wound between the ribs, he made a considerable wound in the heart as he was removing the surrounding tissue, failing also to notice the other smaller wound made by the thrust between the ribs. However, before dismissing him as a poor surgeon, it is interesting to look carefully at what Nairn said when he did discover the stab wound between the ribs. In Curtis's account of his evidence, he was reported as saying:

> I next examined the external surface of the ribs, and ... discovered a wound

The *Sunday Times* report was similar; but in the inquest evidence as detailed in the prosecution brief, and the reports of the trial evidence in *The Times*, *The Standard*, the *Morning*

*Chronicle* and *The Observer*, his words were: 'I examined the *internal* surface of the ribs [author's italics]'. It may be that the external surface of the chest was in an advanced state of decay which would have made finding a stab wound difficult. The internal surface would have had some degree of protection, and as has been mentioned, Nairn had commented on its good state of preservation. Since he knew exactly where to look from the cut in the shift, he was able to locate the wound on the inside of the chest cavity with relative ease.

The broad consensus among the three surgeons, although Chaplin was equivocal, was that the damage caused by the gunshot wound to the head would probably have been insufficient to have killed Maria; Nairn suggested later that it should not have produced the considerable effusion of blood which Corder maintained had happened. But even a superficial glance at the layout of arteries in the head shows that the maxilliary artery, together with its branches and associated veins, lies close to the area where the pistol ball is supposed to have entered the head, 'through the left cheek removing the last two grinders'. The path of the shot was determined from damage to the bone after the latter had been thoroughly cleaned, but damage to the soft tissue was not determined. Lawton, who conducted the original examination, commented in reference to the injury to the face, on the 'state of decomposition' in which he found it. It never seemed to have occurred to any of the surgeons that even if the maxilliary artery (or any other major blood-vessel) was not directly in the path of the pistol ball, one of the teeth or a bone fragment shattered by the ball and acting like shrapnel could have severed the artery or one of its branches, fatally wounding Maria, and causing the bleeding that Corder claimed had happened.

Curtis, who seemed to be unaware of the *Sunday Times* revelation, was sufficiently concerned with the problem of the stab wounds and Corder's denial of responsibility, that he wrote to Mr Orridge seeking 'the most recent information'. Orridge's reply, on 26 August 1828, nine days after the newspaper story, is very interesting:

> With regard to the confession ... it may be perhaps ... partial ... but ... he never denied any of the offences of which he was suspected or charged, or declared himself innocent;– his expressions were, 'O spare me; the public must be satisfied with what I have confessed,' thereby meaning, as I understand it, *spare me the recital*. I confess, from his having always denied the stabs, &c. and from his never having denied anything else, I am inclined to believe him in that particular.

Orridge supplied further evidence to support that conclusion; he overheard Corder, who could not have known he was being overheard, talking to another prisoner:

> If the story of the stabs is sworn to by the surgeon it will go near to hang me; but they had nothing to do with her death, for she died instantaneously from the pistol.

Furthermore, Corder repeated this to the chaplain and other prisoners well before the trial. Orridge said that Corder had spoken to him saying:

> O, Sir, the mistaken opinions of the surgeons about those wounds might have hung an innocent man

Orridge finished his letter to Curtis:

> From his never having declared himself innocent in any other particular, I cannot see any motive he could have for denying this.[8]

So the prison governor was saying that he believed William Corder when he denied stabbing Maria! If that were the case, then he was endorsing the view that the 'stab-wounds' were caused either by the enthusiastic juryman or during the disinterment.

There was no further press comment, and the general consensus seemed to be that Corder was lying respecting the stab wounds. But the story about the juryman and his 'conscientious curiosity' must have come from somewhere and was, apparently, believed by the prison governor who may well have instigated an investigation. Corder had been hanged, and although there was plenty of damning circumstantial evidence against him, the decision of the jury may have revolved around the fact that if Maria had shot herself, she could not possibly have stabbed herself as well. If it now emerged that Corder really was telling the truth, and he hadn't stabbed her – notwithstanding the lie about the pistol – fingers might start to point at the coroner for having failed to conduct the inquest properly and control his jury; the judge and jury in the trial might also come under suspicion for convicting a man on spurious evidence. If someone on the inquest jury really *had* been responsible for the stab wounds, they were hardly going to admit it and be accused of subverting the trial of the year.

The evidence from the inquest and trial revealed that Maria's body had been placed doubled up in a sack and was lying on its right side. That being the case, the probing of the ground by Thomas Martin with his mole-spike could not have caused the 'thrust in the [right] eye' which left the impression of a sharp point in the sphenoidal sinus. The exact position of the wound in the neck was not mentioned, so it is impossible to speculate whether the mole-spike could have caused it, but it could have caused the thrust between the ribs on the left side of the body which was uppermost. Thomas Martin thought that he had injured the body in the thigh, and it is clear that when a body is doubled up, the thigh would be close to the chest. On the other hand the surgeons stated that the thrust between the ribs appeared to have been made with a blade, narrow at the sharp edge with a broad back; the story of the enthusiastic juror probing the body to establish the extent of putridity is quite compelling.

# *Respice*

**W**hat really happened between William Corder and Maria Martin in the Red Barn? Some facts are indisputable. William Corder claimed that he shot her there during a struggle and then buried the body but he always denied stabbing her; on the question of strangulation he said that he 'may' have dragged the body through the barn by the handkerchief around the neck. According to the three surgeons, Maria's body definitely showed signs of at least three stab wounds, and explanations of how these might have come about have been given in the last chapter; the prison governor, Mr Orridge, seemed to have believed Corder when he denied stabbing Maria. It has also been pointed out that Thomas Martin's probing with his mole spike must have significantly injured the body, and that that injury was never reported by any of the surgeons.

Was it murder or manslaughter? Some of the newspaper reports insisted that Maria's death was premeditated murder. It was claimed that the grave had already been dug and Corder lured Maria to the barn where she was to change out of her disguise. But the fact that he went to borrow a spade and was seen with a pickaxe later in the afternoon suggests that he really did dig the grave after he had killed Maria, and furthermore that he had been unprepared to do so. But if Corder didn't intend to kill her, why was he carrying loaded pistols? Corder was short, short-sighted, relatively slight of build and frequently carried large amounts of money around with him; he was very probably afraid of being robbed.

The obvious answer to the charge of premeditated murder is the one Corder himself gave in court. Would he really have taken Maria to the Red Barn with the intention of murdering her there, when Maria's stepmother, stepbrother and sister all saw them off and knew where they were going, and also knew that he had a pistol that he told them was loaded – although he obviously forgot the latter point in his defence statement? Possibly he really did intend to wait until he got Maria somewhere out in the country and then kill her and bury her body in the fields – as he had done with their child – but their violent argument precipitated the deed. The question remains, why would he have done so knowing that if Maria did disappear, several people knew that it was with him that she was last seen?

If it was premeditated murder, what was the motive? Their child was dead, so there was no financial liability against William. Even if he had promised to marry Maria and then changed his mind, no court in the land would have convicted him of breach of promise when the complainant was the mother of three illegitimate children by three different fathers. One suggestion was that Corder really did murder their child and he then killed Maria to prevent her exposing him to the authorities. But the Martins insisted that the child was sickly and subject to fits, and in any case, William and Maria would hardly be arguing over a five-pound note if she thought that he had murdered their son. Even so in September 1828, the *Bath Chronicle* reported:

> it be the fact, that Corder confessed that, with the privity
> of Maria Martin, he murdered the child.[1]

Nevertheless, Maria did have a hold of sorts over William. There was the question of concealing the birth of their baby and its clandestine burial. Both William and Maria were equally guilty over that and each could have received a sentence of between one and two years in prison, but the source of friction between them seemed to be Maria's concern that the child's grave would be found and the consequences to herself. Much more serious was the theft of the five-pound note. The punishment for that depended on the circumstances – theft from the post carried the death penalty although that sentence was usually limited to employees of the Post Office. At the very least the offence was embezzlement, which could result in transportation for seven or fourteen years. In fact Maria had already perjured herself by writing to the Post Office to say that she had, after all, received the five-pound note although she could claim coercion, and there were witnesses at the bank who could have identified William Corder. If Maria told the authorities either about the clandestine burial or the missing five-pound note she would incriminate herself and likely end up in prison. This would have been clear to both of them, so the possibility of Maria 'talking' seems a very weak motive for murder.

Much more likely is that it really was a crime of passion. Corder said that Maria flew into a rage in the barn over the dead child, the five-pound note and her feeling that she was not good enough for his family. That is entirely consistent with the evidence of Ann Martin regarding relations between William and Maria before they left the cottage. It seems likely that a violent argument led to a struggle, and in the heat of the moment Corder drew his gun and shot Maria, which is what he said happened. But was that manslaughter or murder? He drew the gun which he knew was loaded; this much he admitted. If he then fired, which he also admitted, it is a moot point as to whether that was not murder; he could not just take the gun from his pocket and pull the trigger, it would have to have been cocked first which might have been difficult if they were 'scuffling' as Corder claimed. Of course the provocation could have been extreme; he might have been too ashamed to repeat some of the things Maria said to him in her rage.

Was there any other evidence of murderous intent not used in court? Curtis reproduced many anecdotes in his book. Some are consistent with other evidence, some might be true and some are unlikely. One story that seems unlikely, and yet Curtis insists it was told to him by Maria's stepmother following detailed questioning, concerns an apparent attempt by William Corder to poison Maria's little boy Thomas Henry. This report was repeated by several newspapers, where it was stated that the originator of the story was Maria's father.[2] Apparently, while Maria was away from the cottage, William arrived first with a fig and then a baked pear for Thomas Henry. Both, he refused to eat. When Mrs Martin opened them up to see if she could tempt him with the soft inner parts, she claimed to have found a 'pill' in each fruit. These she threw away so there was no question of any analysis. Furthermore, it was reported that when the policeman Lea asked Corder about the allegation, he did not deny it. It seems an improbable story, except that Curtis says that he questioned Ann Martin carefully about the circumstances. In England, figs and pears are ripe in late summer, so if the incident did occur, it must have been August or September time. In August 1826, not long after William and Maria became lovers, Thomas Henry would have been one year and eight months old, probably old enough to be tempted by edible treats. Ripe figs are one of the sweetest fruits in existence, so it could have enticed the child, but what was the motive? Did William want Thomas Henry out of the way so that he could spend more time with Maria? The following year, August 1827, Thomas Henry was two years and eight months and would have been even more susceptible to sweet things. Maria was dead and buried in the Red Barn, but William had just exchanged the letters with Peter Mathews where he effectively admitted to embezzlement. Was it therefore a really nasty attempt on Corder's part at revenge, or was it all just a piece of embroidered nonsense circulated to blacken his character?

The evidence points to a blazing row erupting in the barn over the buried child, the stolen five-pound note and Maria's exasperation with William thinking she was not good enough for his family. A struggle ensued, and William pulled his gun from his pocket in the heat of the moment and shot Maria in the face. As far as the law stood at the time, William might have been able to have pleaded extreme provocation and got away with his life. The fact that he lied in court in his defence statement about having a gun with him and had already made numerous attempts to conceal what had happened, means that the guilty verdict and sentence were almost inevitable, even without the evidence of the stab wounds.

So much for William Corder, but was he the only one responsible for Maria's death? The reaction of most people to the Red Barn affair is acute scepticism regarding Ann Martin's dreams, the dreams which led to the discovery of Maria's body. Prophetic dreams work well in Gothic or romantic novels, but can it be believed that in real life it is possible for a dream to foretell with such accuracy both that a murder has been committed and the location of the body? Most of the recent accounts of the murder suggest that Ann Martin's explanation of how she knew where Maria was buried stretches credibility to breaking point; she must, it is claimed, have been in some way complicit. Her account was never questioned during Corder's trial, although in the extensive press coverage of the affair, several newspapers expressed elements of disbelief. Reactions from people 'on the spot' were reported in *The Times*:

> Some believe in the story of the dream to its full extent; others reject that part which relates to the particular spot being pointed out, while some few repudiate the dream altogether.[3]

Ann Martin was still a young and apparently attractive woman in 1827; she was 35 years old, only nine years older than Maria and more than twenty years younger than her husband. A theory first expounded by Gibbs and Maltby, suggested that

Ann was fed up with her much older husband and grew to be infatuated with William Corder.[4] Because of his relationship with Maria, he was a frequent visitor to the cottage, and he and Ann became embroiled in a relationship. Jealousy then raised its head. Maria had fine clothes and few responsibilities other than little Thomas Henry who was being supported financially by Peter Mathews. Ann had to keep house for her husband Thomas, as well as Maria, Maria's sister Ann and half-brother George, two more of her own children and an elder brother of Maria's. She would also have had to look after Thomas Henry during Maria's frequent absences. She did not have the fine clothes that Maria possessed although she may have coveted them, and Maria's clothes were the subject of rows. Gibbs and Maltby suggested that Ann encouraged Corder to lure Maria to the barn and kill her; the way would then be open for them to enjoy a relatively unencumbered love affair. It was further suggested that when Corder first moved to London, he sent Ann money to keep her quiet, and then the supply dwindled. When she found out about his marriage, she invented the dreams in order to vent her spite on him. As far as it goes, it is a credible theory and does explain how she knew where the body was buried.

But there are several problems with this hypothesis, the most obvious being that apart from the dreams, there is no evidence that Ann was 'involved' with Corder. If they had been having an affair and Ann was complicit in the murder, and he then left for London, the last thing he would tell her is that he had got married to someone else. No-one in Polstead knew of Corder's marriage until after his arrest except George Gardiner, whom Curtis implied knew; he stated that when Gardiner told his brother-in-law, Ayres, of Corder's address in London, he said that if he would

[call] at No 6 Gray's Inn Terrace, he would find a person with whom the prisoner had formed a connection in London[5]

It could be argued that Ann acted out of spite after Corder went to London, apparently abandoning her; that cannot be ruled out, although such an action could easily backfire. If Ann really was involved in Maria's murder, even if Corder had just told her about it after the event and she did not report it, she was an accessory. And if, by her actions, she condemned Corder to the gallows, he would hardly fail to implicate her. At the very least she would have got prison or transportation; worst case, she could have accompanied William Corder on his last journey.

There is no evidence to suggest that Ann Martin was any different from what she appeared to be: a conscientious mother and stepmother with a full household to look after and an ongoing worry about a wayward and flighty stepdaughter of whom she was probably very fond. At the age of 20 Ann had married a much older man, taking on his three children.* Having done that, she bore him three more children and was still living with him in 1851, nearly twenty-five years after the Red Barn affair when she was 58 and he was 80.[6] Almost certainly, she continued to look after Thomas in his old age until his death in 1854. Ann Martin does not fit the profile of a jealous and adulterous woman who would conspire in the murder of her own stepdaughter.

How then are the dreams to be explained? Ann Martin claimed that she had first dreamed before Christmas 1827 that Maria had been murdered and buried in the Red Barn. The last time anyone had seen Maria was on Friday 18 May 1827. She was crying quite probably because she had to leave her 'beautiful little boy', Thomas Henry, and he had refused to kiss her not recognizing her in disguise. According to Ann and Thomas Martin, she had been crying when she brought her dying infant, William Corder's child, into their bedroom, and Curtis reported that Maria was a good and conscientious mother. How then could a complete absence of any written

---

\* Maria's two younger sisters, Hannah and Jemima, had died in infancy.

word after more than six months be explained, let alone a visit to her little boy? Considering the strength of bond between mother and child, something that Ann Martin understood, she may have reasoned that only forcible restraint or death could explain the complete lack of contact. Corder's final letter had been dated 18 October, five months after Maria had last been seen. Since then there had been no word at all. Corder had behaved suspiciously; Ann's son George had seen him walking between his home and the Red Barn with a pickaxe over his shoulder on the afternoon he and Maria were supposed to be going to Ipswich, but he denied it saying it must have been Tom Akers, yet George was sure it was him. Ann Martin saw him the next day, Saturday afternoon, at his mother's house. How had he transacted his business with Maria in Ipswich, fifteen miles or so by road, so quickly that he was able to be home again so soon? There was the incident of Maria's umbrella which Corder had with him at his brother's funeral. When Ann asked him about it he said it belonged to someone else, but then later on changed his story and said that it was Maria's and she had lent it to him. And of course, when William and Maria left the Martins' cottage, he had at least one loaded pistol with him.

It is not surprising that Ann Martin worried about Maria's disappearance and it seems likely that the worry preyed on her mind and translated itself into dreams. Curtis said that he had 'frequent conversations' with Mrs Martin on the subject of the dreams; she commented:

> Corder, Maria and the Red Barn occupied many of [my] waking thoughts, and became a topic of daily conversation.[7]

But why the Red Barn rather than burial somewhere in the fields? Ann may have reasoned that murder in the open air can always be observed. Even in the remote countryside, as Polstead was and still is, one never knows who is about; Corder was unaware that he was observed by George Martin when he was walking home with the pickaxe. Being inside the barn with the door locked would be the perfect place to commit a murder with plenty of time to dig a grave unobserved. All of these things Ann Martin may well have imagined and worried about. Every time she looked at little Thomas Henry, who would have been with her most of the time, she must have thought of Maria. Little wonder then, that those worries found their way into her dreams.

The other candidate for conspiracy theorists is Samuel 'Beauty' Smith alias Cooper. Smith was a local miscreant and known associate of William Corder; they had conspired together in the stealing of a pig. Smith was first mentioned in several newspaper reports published on 2 May 1828. The press seemed to have had a permanent correspondent at the Lambeth Street Police Office with its sitting magistrates, and anything of interest was recorded and published. On this occasion Lea, the police officer who had arrested Corder, produced a 'dirk' or small sword that he had taken from Grove House at Ealing. During the reconvened inquest on Maria Martin a few days before, one of the witnesses, Robert Offord, confirmed that Corder had, the previous year, brought in for sharpening a small sword with a curved blade, and a brass-mounted white handle. Lea remembered seeing such an item at Corder's house when he was arrested but did not impound it at the time. He went back for it and now produced it as evidence to the sitting Magistrates, Messrs Wyatt and Mathias. They freely discussed the Red Barn affair, firstly mentioning the attempt Corder had apparently made to poison Thomas Henry. It was on this occasion that Lea said that he had asked Corder about the alleged attempt to poison the child and he had not denied it. Mr Wyatt then asked Lea:

Do you know what are the grounds of suspicion against Smith?

Lea answered:

> I understand that Smith has been frequently heard to
> say, previous to his own apprehension, that he could
> hang Corder whenever he pleased. Smith is at present
> on board one of the convict ships at Portsmouth,
> preparatory to his being sent out of the country.[8]

Curtis clarified who Smith was and why he was implicated:

> At Polstead, there resided a man of the name of Samuel
> Smith, alias Cooper, but commonly called and known
> by the appellation *Beauty Smith*, a notorious thief, who
> had been twice transported in the last sixteen years, for
> pig stealing, and several times imprisoned for minor
> offences.

According to Curtis, constable Ayres, who was investigating
the pig stealing, had accosted Smith saying: 'So, Bill Corder
was in the pig concern with you'. Smith had responded: 'I'll be
damned if he will not be hung one of these days'. Investigation
reveals that Smith really had already been sentenced to be
transported twice, although his first sentence of seven years
was served entirely on the prison hulks at Woolwich. In March
1828, he was convicted at Chelmsford of stealing an ass, and
sentenced to be transported for life. When the story of the Red
Barn murder broke, he was on board another hulk, *Leviathan*,
moored at Portsmouth, awaiting a ship for Australia.

The 'grounds for suspicion against Smith' were his
association with Corder in felonious activities, and his
comments about Corder being hanged. The magistrates sought
permission from the Home Office to have Smith questioned
about the murder and be prevented from leaving the country
until after Corder's trial, in case he should implicate Smith in
some way. He was questioned but denied all knowledge of
Maria Martin, saying that his comments were made in respect
of animal stealing. Corder made no mention of Smith at the

trial or afterwards, and Smith sailed for Australia on board *Royal George* on 26 August 1828. Donald McCormick in his book claimed that it was Smith who actually stabbed Maria to put her out of her misery.[9] His claims have been thoroughly discredited but Beauty Smith remains a fascinating character, and his life and criminal career have been extensively investigated. Appendix 1 contains an account of his various encounters with the law.

Regardless of McCormick's claims, could Smith have been involved in some way? Although he may have been at liberty at the time of Maria's murder, there is no evidence whatsoever to link him to it. Examination of his criminal activities both before and afterwards reveals him to have been a career petty criminal. His speciality was animal stealing and the convictions that resulted in his three separate sentences to be transported are well documented. Even while in Australia, he was sentenced to a year in the penal colony at Newcastle for what was probably petty thieving. But with one exception, there is no recorded offence against him involving violence. The exception, in 1845, which resulted in the cancellation of his Ticket of Leave in New South Wales, was that he 'assaulted and violated one Emma Fletcher alias Ridgeway'. For that offence he was found guilty of common assault and sentenced to two years in prison. The episode with Emma Fletcher, who was around 12 years old, was sickening, but was it symptomatic of a murderous temperament?

All of the evidence suggests that William Corder killed Maria Martin and buried her body in the Red Barn without the involvement of anyone else; Corder confessed as much. In that sense the inquest jury, the coroner, the surgeons, the judge and the trial jury had been correct in their verdicts. But hardly anyone directly involved with the Red Barn affair can have been completely satisfied with the outcome. Thomas Martin wanted justice for his murdered daughter and himself after

171

nearly a year of distress with no news of her, followed by the agony of finding her buried body almost on his own doorstep. The revelation barely a week after Corder had been hanged, that after all he might not have stabbed her, robbed him of the certainty of that closure. Ann Martin too must have felt similar feelings of frustration.

If the *Sunday Times* story is to be believed, Mr Wayman, the coroner/prosecutor, must have felt foolish for the slipshod way he conducted the inquest, not having cautioned the jury about interfering with the body, and failing to have observed someone doing so. If the stabs to the side, neck and head *were* caused by an 'enthusiastic' member of the jury, which seems to be quite likely, then the surgeon who examined the body initially, Mr Lawton, was shown to be incapable of distinguishing between a wound made in life and one made long after death; likewise the two other surgeons who examined the body at the exhumation. Lawton entirely failed to notice the stab in the side when the body was first examined, which made the exhumation necessary, and none of the surgeons identified what must have been an obvious wound caused by Thomas Martin's mole spike. It is clear from the judge's summing up when he questioned whether Maria could have committed suicide by shooting and stabbing herself, that the evidence of the surgeons effectively misled both judge and jury. Corder's defence, that Maria Martin killed herself, was demolished by the evidence of the stab wounds. It was not credible that any person could shoot themselves in the head and then stab themselves in several different places. Given that Corder had confessed to being there and burying the body, the stab wounds, along with his lie about his pistols being kept in his bedroom, were the main evidence against him; all the rest was circumstantial. The defence and prosecution counsel, and the judge, must also have felt rather foolish by the revelation of the post-mortem stabbing of the body.

What was Mr Orridge's reaction to the 'revelation' in the *Sunday Times* that he had instigated an investigation and showed Corder's confession to have been true? He didn't comment on it directly in his letter to Curtis, but in view of his declaration that he believed Corder over the stab wounds, the story may have had more than an element of truth. Possibly he decided that the best thing was to make no further comment. After all, William Corder did admit killing Maria Martin; the right man had been hanged and that was that. If Orridge did carry out an investigation, he may just have been 'tidying up', wanting to demonstrate that, after all, William Corder *had* made a full and complete confession of guilt just before he was hanged.

The two Mrs Corders were grieving for William. Mrs Corder senior had seen her husband and four sons die within three years. William had been her 'best boy'; she must have been heartbroken. William's wife Mary had been bankrupted by the proceedings; his defence costs were in the region of £700 and she had also had to pay back the ninety-three pounds he stole from the bank. With all of that, she was heavily pregnant. But she must have wondered why she was left with a bill for £700 for an entirely botched defence, and her solicitor, Mr Charnock, was to blame for the failed strategy. He was a friend of the Corder family, and he strongly supported the idea of Maria's suicide as William's defence. The eminent and experienced Mr Humphreys, Corder's original solicitor, had been very much against that, to the extent that he refused any further involvement in the case.

Then there was Mr Brodrick the main defence barrister; he was paid 140 guineas *plus expenses* for his two days' work. That is equivalent to around £4,000 per day in modern money. What did Mary Corder get for her 140 guineas? Brodrick seemed incapable of asking the obvious and searching questions. He pressed Maria's stepmother about what she knew regarding the buried child:

173

> Now, woman, on your solemn oath, do you know that it
> was not buried at Sudbury, but that you know when and
> where it was buried?

This was a point hardly relevant to the case, but he then
entirely failed to cross-examine her on the fundamental
burning question: did she really have those dreams? How
was it that she knew where Maria's body had been buried?
He got all hot and bothered about Mr Wayman's questionable
position as coroner and prosecutor, and the fact that Corder
was not present during the examinations at the inquest, but
failed to press Lawton, the first surgeon to examine the body,
regarding how it was he failed to spot the critical stab wound
between the ribs. He railed about the 'exhibitions going about
the neighbourhood, representing Corder as the murderer',
but blustered about there being no proof that the desks at
Grove House where Corder was living were his. He expressed
indignation at the 'dissenting' preacher who had come to
Polstead and given a sermon near the barn where he described
Corder as Maria Martin's murderer, yet knowing William
Corder's vehement denial that he had stabbed Maria, he could
have done far more to press the surgeons regarding the age
of the various stab wounds, particularly when it became clear
that one of the wounds in the heart had been caused by Lawton
during his original examination on the first day of the inquest.
There was Nairn's evidence, when he stated that the large
wound in the heart was recent, whereas the stab between the
ribs – which was supposed to have been what caused the other
wound in the heart – was of 'long duration'. Brodrick could
have pushed Nairn far harder to justify his opinion. He might
also have commented on Lawton removing Maria's head thus
preventing any further examination of the stab in the neck or
the signs of strangulation.

Brodrick's major blunder, assuming that he advised
Corder on his defence statement which he must have done,

considering that several very good legal points were made in it, was to fail to spot Corder's obvious falsehood that the pistols were normally kept in his bedroom and that Maria must have stolen them when she was there. Corder said in his defence statement that Maria had shot herself with one of the pistols, and he found the other one in her bag. He had not missed them from his room as he had 'no occasion to use the[m]'. But Ann Martin and her son and stepdaughter had already stated, quite clearly, that Corder had at least one loaded pistol with him when he and Maria went to the Red Barn. That was on the first day of the trial, so there was plenty of time to adjust the defence statement overnight. Neither Brodrick nor Prendergast, nor the solicitor, Charnock, noticed that gaffe; if there had been any doubt in the jury's mind, that lie would surely have tipped the balance.

Brodrick's performance was pitiful. It is doubtful whether he spent any more time reading the papers on the case than during the coach trip to Bury. William Brodrick was a rich man who had inherited a considerable fortune from his uncle. At the age of forty-four he was probably at the height of his powers; he died not long after the Corder trial, and his obituary in the *Legal Observer* of 1830 paints a picture of him as a very successful barrister. He first made his name in the trial of the Cato Street conspirators in 1820, where he was said to have defended,* and the trial of Henry Fauntleroy for embezzling a considerable sum of money, which according to a contemporary account of the case was in excess of £400,000. Brodrick led a ferociously complex appeal against Fauntleroy's conviction, which failed, and the latter was hanged in November 1824. Nevertheless, it was said that Brodrick was in great demand initially at the Old Bailey, and latterly at Hertford and Chelmsford. From the *Legal Observer*:

---

* The 'defence' was unsuccessful, although there seems to be no newspaper record of Brodrick being involved.

175

of [Brodrick's] talents, perhaps his great success at the bar is the best criterion; his knowledge of the law, was ... extensive and deep ... In the conduct of a cause he was firm, zealous and undaunted: he always regarded the success of his client as his paramount object, and no exertions were spared by him which tended towards its attainment.[10]

Perhaps so, but the Corder case was definitely the exception that proved the rule.

# *Epilogue*

In death as in the last few months of his life, William Corder achieved a notoriety almost as intense as any other criminal in British legal history. As directed by the judge, his body was dissected, a death mask was made and his head was phrenologically analysed to 'correctly identify' his criminal tendencies. The death mask resides at Norwich Castle with a copy at the Moyses Hall Museum. His skeleton, minus the original skull, ended up at the West Suffolk General Hospital where it was used for teaching. It then found its way to the Hunterian Museum at the Royal College of Surgeons. In 2004, Linda Nessworthy, distantly related to Corder, persuaded the museum to release the remains which were then cremated and the ashes buried in Polstead churchyard. A 'ghost hunter', R Thurston Hopkins, claimed that Corder's skull was removed and polished and kept in a box. Following some alleged 'bad luck', the skull was buried in an unknown Suffolk churchyard.[1] Other parts of Corder's body were not so lucky. Part of his skin was tanned and used to bind a copy of Curtis's book; his scalp with part of an ear also remain. Both items are currently on show in the Moyses Hall Museum at Bury St Edmunds.

Maria Martin, having been buried and exhumed twice, was finally laid to rest in Polstead churchyard on 19 May 1828. A curious story appeared in the *Morning Chronicle* some months later, to the effect that the Rector of Polstead, John Whitmore, had declared that a stone to Maria Martin's memory should never be erected over her grave 'while he had the power to prevent it'.[2] He considered that such a monument would simply 'keep it alive in the public mind'. It is notable that Mr Whitmore seemed to distance himself from the events surrounding two of his parishioners. A stone was subsequently erected over Maria's grave, and this may have happened after 1841 when Whitmore was succeeded by James Coyte. Such was the continuing interest in the Red Barn affair that visitors to Maria's grave sought a souvenir of the event by chipping a piece from the gravestone.[3] Eventually the stone was entirely demolished and all that remains in the graveyard today is a wooden notice attached to a shed with the legend:

> Near this place lie the remains of Maria Marten who died in the Red Barn Polstead and was buried on April 20th 1828 aged 26 years R I P

William Corder's tragically reduced family continued to dwindle. In January 1829, less than six months after his death, his eldest sister, Mary Borham, died at the age of 41 depriving Mrs Corder senior of the fifth of her children in a period of just two years. In 1831 Mrs Corder decided to give up farming, and the contents of the farm, horses, cows and pigs, along with wagons, ploughs and other tools of the farming trade were put up for auction. Her one remaining daughter, Elizabeth, evidently decided that she wanted to distance herself from the Corder name. In April 1829 at the age of 34, she married Martin Harvey in Wakes Colne, Essex.

Of all of the surviving players in the Red Barn drama, it was William Corder's wife Mary whose life was completely turned upside down by the affair. In November 1827 she had been an independent woman with property running a girls' boarding school in London and had never heard of William Corder. Nine months later she was the widow of an executed murderer, bankrupt and heavily pregnant. Some people at least recognized her plight. The *Bury and Norwich Post* published a letter on 27 August, two weeks after the execution, calling the public's attention to the plight of Corder's widow:

I do not attempt to palliate the impropriety of conduct which has led to such deplorable misfortunes, but I would ask, whether these have not been punishment sufficiently severe? ... She is about to become a mother, and it is understood in utter want of comforts ... let not English, much less Christian women, refuse their assistance in this her hour of bodily extremity.

With the letter was enclosed a sovereign, and several others made similar contributions. Not everyone was as charitable; in September, the *Suffolk Herald* published a correspondent with a very different view:

Some weak or ill-advised person attempted in a contemporary print of last week, to promote a subscription for the wife of the executed murderer, Corder, on the plea that she impoverished herself by the expenses of the trial ... This woman, when Miss Moore, received from a thoughtless young man, £300 forfeit for not completing a proposal of marriage ... In the course of the trial she was to be seen, daily, flaunting about Bury as if to provoke observation: in the prospect of his death she ordered as expensive a suit of widow's weeds as could be procured ... We should like to know ... if her main object was not to secure the little property which was to fall to her husband's share[4]

The story about the breach of promise payment was not true; it had been aired extensively in the press in the run-up to the trial and Mrs Corder had 'vigorously' denied it. The *Suffolk Herald* reported that it was a

cousin of Mrs Corder's who recovered £300 [possibly £500] in a court of law from a gentleman for a breach of promise of marriage.[5]

In the first instance at least, Mary Corder's mother-in-law took her in, and her child, John Corder, was born at the Corder house in Polstead on 16 November 1828; he was christened on 12 December. It would be nice to think that the two Mrs Corders were able to provide each other mutual support and comfort, mourning the loss of son and husband and caring together for the one tangible element of him that remained, i.e. his son. There is no record of the sequence of events, but it all went horribly wrong at some point, and inevitably it was money that was the cause.

Seven years later, a case was pleaded at the Court of Chancery, that place of 'expense, delay and despair'. In Corder v Harvey and others, January 1835, Mary Corder sought payment of that part of William Corder's father's will that was due.[6] William had initially made over his share of his father's will to his mother-in-law, Mrs Moore, in exchange for £200. It was normal practice to do this for a person of property about to be tried for a crime, the conviction for which would brand the person a felon. Under English law, any assets possessed of a felon reverted to the Crown. Normally, property and money would be made over to friends or family before the trial. In this case, Corder chose his mother-in-law rather than his mother or sisters, possibly to ensure that his wife and child would get the benefit of his inheritance, more likely because having already embezzled hundreds of pounds from the farm, his mother and sisters would have refused to give him any more money. Payment for the transferred property, 'a consideration', was a legal requirement, and the money would have been given directly to his wife who would have spent it on the costs of his defence. Mrs Moore had an interview with Mrs Corder senior regarding the amount William Corder was due under his father's will. The accounts were 'not made up', but it was claimed that Mrs Corder senior told Mrs Moore that William's share would be around £500, whereupon Mrs Moore upped the consideration paid to £500.

Mrs Moore died and in her will left everything, including William Corder's share of the benefit of his father's will, to her daughter, Mary Corder.* Frequent representations were made to Mary Corder senior for a settlement of the will. She (Mrs Corder senior), claimed she had paid Mrs Moore the money due and had received a receipt; Mrs Corder junior claimed it was fraudulent. In a deposition to the court she insisted that Mrs Corder senior, her daughter Mary Borham†, son-in-law Jeremiah Borham, daughter Elizabeth and son-in-law Martin Harvey conspired together to split the proceeds of the will, and pass the livestock and assets of the Corders' farm to Elizabeth and her husband who were farming at Little Tey. A solicitor's letter was sent threatening action in Chancery. The response was that the settlement of the will was proper, Mrs Moore had been paid a settlement and had given a receipt and Mrs Corder junior would get nothing more until after the decease of Mrs Corder senior.‡ No notice would be taken of any further communications. A subsequent solicitor's letter was returned unanswered. Mary Corder junior instigated the costly Chancery case in order to force her mother-in-law, and the other co-legatees to pay William Corder's share of the legacy to her as the rightful heir to his portion of his father's estate.

The case stalled because although Martin and Elizabeth Harvey responded to Mary Corder's bill, as did Jeremiah Borham, Mrs Corder senior did not. Mrs Corder senior was the executrix of the will, so without her response the case could not proceed. What happened next is illustrated by an action that was heard at the Chelmsford Assizes in March 1836. Mary

---

\* In a letter to his mother from prison, William admitted that only a 'small sum' from his father's will would be due to his wife, perhaps acknowledging that he had already embezzled a considerable amount of money from the estate.

† Mrs Corder junior was apparently unaware that Mary Borham had died in early 1829

‡ Payments would be due after Mrs Corder senior's death, in respect of her husband's and son's wills.

Corder junior charged Martin Harvey, Thomas Harvey and Mark Gyant with trespass and false imprisonment. The alleged offences had taken place the previous August, 1835.

Following Mrs Corder senior's failure to respond to the Chancery bill, an attachment was issued from the court to be served on her. She could not be found. A second attachment was issued in August, and Mrs Corder junior accompanied the county official, Mr Green, to ensure that it was delivered. They went to the house where Mrs Corder's daughter Elizabeth lived with her husband, Martin Harvey, in Little Tey near Colchester, where the junior Mrs Corder suspected her mother-in-law was hiding. Eventually Martin Harvey allowed the court officer to search the house; it was established to Green's satisfaction that Mrs Corder senior, now sixty-nine years old, was not there. The junior Mrs Corder was not happy, and

> seated herself in a field opposite the house, where she
> continued watching the whole of that night ... in order to
> observe if her mother-in-law escaped

The following day, a Sunday, she was still there and she invited passers-by to join her and 'protect her'. Between fifty and a hundred persons did so. That evening there was an incident when one of the assembled number struck a horse pulling a chaise with two visitors on board leaving the house. Mrs Corder refused to leave when asked and Martin Harvey, who was a constable, assisted by his brother Thomas Harvey and Gyant, 'arrested' her and took her to the Six Bells at Great Tey where she was to be confined until a magistrate could be found. Apparently the magistrate told Harvey that she could be set free but she refused to leave without a magistrates hearing. Finally on the Wednesday she did leave.

The judge summing up said that Mrs Corder had 'mediated' a breach of the peace, but the jury returned a verdict in her favour and awarded her twenty pounds damages.[7] Mrs Corder senior never responded to the Chancery case and it did not come to court. She died five years later at Horse Heath in Cambridgeshire.[8] Mary Corder and her son, John Corder, who was now 8 years old, were left effectively penniless. Any money she had left would have been expended in the Chancery case. The Court of Chancery was a notorious sink for money; her submission to the court consisted of five pages of parchment, each one 29 inches wide by 25 inches long with 70 lines of closely written script in lengthy legalese. It was her last chance to get her in-laws to honour the will of William's father, John Corder, and explains her desperation to force her mother-in-law to respond; without that response, the case could not come to judgement. The extent of Mary Corder's situation was made clear eleven years later by an article in the *Essex Standard* in 1847. Some friends of hers had initiated an appeal on her behalf. It said that Mrs Corder

> is now in the deepest distress, her mind being in some degree affected by her severe affliction, and being also a sufferer from almost total deafness.[9]

John Corder, her son, was 'deficient in intellect and his right side is paralyzed'. He had never been able to work. Mary Corder had supported them for some time by 'hemming cravats ... and letting lodgings'. She was unable to continue to do this because of the state of her health and she and her son were 'both in want of clothing and means to procure food'. There was no follow-up story; presumably Mary Corder was afforded some relief, but a few months later the most extraordinary case was reported in the *Essex Standard*. Mary Corder brought an action against 'Elizabeth Harvey and Husband' for 'assault, and damage to property and character'. She alleged that

> [she] had been forcibly dragged out of her dwelling; her furniture broken, and placed in the road; the fruit and vegetables of her garden destroyed, and her character injured by the circulation of slanderous reports

The case was never concluded because Elizabeth Harvey's husband could not be found; he had

> left the neighbourhood about last March, and has not
> since returned, nor was Mrs Harvey at all cognizant of
> his present abode.[10]

It is difficult to know what to make of this report. Had Mary Corder descended into paranoia, convinced that her sister-in-law was out to get her, or was there some truth in the allegation? It was slightly suspicious that in the same way that the Chancery case had been scuppered by Mrs Corder senior being unable to be found, so this case too failed because of the disappearance of one of the defendants. Neither Elizabeth nor her husband can be identified in subsequent census returns so what became of them is unknown.

Mary Corder only appears twice more in press reports. The following year, 1848, she was reported as being unsuccessful in obtaining a pension from the *Governesses' Benevolent Fund*; the report, half of which was taken up with details of her condition, reported that 'her own mind suffered so severely that she can scarcely attend to her own maintenance'.[11] Nine years later, in 1857, the *Essex Standard* reported that on 17 June, Mary Corder, aged 61, 'the widow of the late William Corder, formerly of Polstead, Suffolk', had died.[12]

Maria Martin's little boy, Thomas Henry Martin, grew up being looked after by his grandparents. It is to be hoped that his father, Peter Mathews, continued to support him while he was young and Curtis claimed that Mathews intended to pay for a proper education. Census returns indicate that Thomas Henry worked as an agricultural labourer, so it seems unlikely that Mathews made good his promise. In July 1842, Peter Mathews married Harriet Hone; he was 56, she was 35. They had four children. Mathews died in Brighton in 1870 leaving £18,000 to his family with no mention in his will of his son Thomas Henry Martin.[13]

The *Bury and Norwich Post*, on 8 July 1829, reported that Thomas Martin visited the hospital where William Corder's skeleton had been put on show together with the pistol with which he shot Maria, and deposited a shilling in the collecting box. Thomas and Ann Martin continued to live in the same cottage until Thomas died in 1854 aged 84. When Ann died a few years later in June 1858, Thomas Henry inherited the cottage at a nominal rent of one shilling a year. In February 1861, he married Isabella Woods, a dressmaker, in Polstead; he was 36, she was 42; they had no children.

A quarter of a century later, the *Ipswich Journal* of 2 December 1887 ran a piece, 'Reminiscences of the "Red Barn" Murder'. It reported the verdict of an inquest held on Thomas Henry Martin, Maria Martin's son. The newspaper used the report to recall details of the Red Barn murder that had taken place sixty years previously. 'There are a few ... now living who remember the circumstance'. One person, it said, remembered going to school with the murderer; another, the 'young farmer talking sweet nonsense' to Maria in her garden. Yet another remembered a little boy telling his teacher that his grandmother had had a strange dream, following which the body of his mother was found in the barn.

The circumstances of Thomas's death were distressing. His wife, Isabella was 68 years old and a bedridden invalid; Thomas was unable to work and consequently they were very poor. He complained that his head was in a 'very bad state' and his wife did not see him after the Wednesday evening. On Thursday morning she heard him fall over several times in the next room but was unable to get up and help him. She called out for assistance but no-one came. She heard him groaning until Friday morning when he stopped. Finally someone knocked on the door between nine and ten o'clock and Thomas was found dead on the floor.

John Corder, William Corder's posthumous son, may have suffered from some sort of paralysis, but his mind was sufficiently sound that he was able to succeed in business. He became a bookseller and newsagent in Colchester where he was well known as a local 'character', although he did eventually end up in the Essex lunatic asylum where he died in 1892. He led an interesting life, and his story is related in Appendix 2.

The famous Red Barn whose name defines Maria Martin's murder, was burned to the ground on 26 December 1842. Several years later, Samuel Stow, who lived with his father in the cottage closest to the barn, was accused of being responsible. Stow was the son of Francis and Phoebe Stow who had given evidence for the prosecution in William Corder's trial; Phoebe Stow had lent Corder one of her husband's spades with which he attempted to dig Maria Martin's grave. Samuel Stow was seen running from the barn the night it was burned down, but the evidence against him was

> made up entirely of statements proved to have been made to different persons by the prisoner, when in gaol for poaching.

The assize jury at Bury St Edmunds declined to believe that testimony and Stow was acquitted; he was, however, found guilty of sending a threatening letter to a Polstead farmer, and was transported for ten years.[14]

History has branded William Corder a murderer, and in the *Oxford Dictionary of National Biography*, that collection of 'people who have shaped the history of the British Isles and beyond', Corder appears with around a hundred others whose principal or sole claim to fame was that they committed the crime of murder. The incriminating circumstantial evidence against him, along with his confession, suggests that he really did kill Maria Martin, although it seems unlikely that it was a premeditated affair. Some of Corder's subsequent actions, and the different stories he told people following the killing, point to a young man of rather limited intelligence; inevitably events caught up with him and he paid the ultimate price. In reality he may have been more of a stupid boy than a scheming, cold-blooded murderer.

Maria Martin was an unknown 25-year-old when she died, remarkable only for the fact that in her short life she had managed to attract three relatively prosperous lovers, and had produced a child with each of them. Within days of the discovery of her body, she became known throughout the country; the circumstances of her life and death inspired peepshows, puppet shows and broadsheets at the time, together with books and plays, and subsequently musicals, TV programmes and films, and these continue to the present day. Maria has attained an iconic place in history as a beautiful young maiden foully done to death in her prime by a cruel, lustful and dissolute young man. If the reality is a little more complex, the legend will ensure that her name lives on, forever associated with the Red Barn in Polstead where she met her untimely end.

## Appendix 1 – Beauty Smith

This is an edited version of an article that appeared in *Genealogists' Magazine*, Vol 31, No4, June 2014.

In the section in his book on William Corder's background, J Curtis described Samuel Smith:

> At Polstead there resided a man of the name Samuel Smith alias Cooper ... [known as] *Beauty* Smith ... a notorious thief who had been twice transported within the last sixteen years for pig-stealing ... This desperado returned home a short time before the sudden disappearance of Maria Marten

'Beauty' Smith was a known associate of William Corder. He was a petty thief who specialized in stealing farm animals. Curtis described how Corder had been involved with Smith in the stealing of a pig. By the time of Corder's trial however, Smith had been convicted in Chelmsford of stealing an ass, and was sentenced to be transported for life. He was on board *Leviathan*, a prison hulk at Portsmouth, awaiting a ship for New South Wales. At the behest of the magistrates concerned with the Red Barn affair, he was questioned as to whether he had any knowledge of Maria Martin's murder. It had been reported that Smith had frequently alluded to Corder, opining that he 'would be hanged one day or the other'. He denied all knowledge of Maria Martin and claimed that his comments on William Corder were purely in respect of the pig-stealing episode. Curtis's book had claimed that Smith had already been transported twice for various offences, and as this seemed to be unlikely, it was appropriate to look at his history.

From Smith's different prison records, his year of birth can be deduced as variously 1765, 1773, 1777, 1778 and 1780. The mean of these is 1775. Identifying with any confidence the provenance of Samuel Smith is probably impossible; certainly it is beyond the scope of the present investigation. There were Smiths (and Coopers) in Polstead, but no Samuel Smith born in the date range of interest. There was a Samuel Smith christened in Nayland in February 1774, and another in Hitcham in July 1777. Nayland is the next but one parish to Polstead and Hitcham is also quite close. Both fathers were also Samuels, and this is interesting because the *Bury and Norwich Post*, on 22 April 1801 reported:

> At the quarter sessions [in Norwich], Samuel Smith, senior was convicted of stealing two hogs, the property of John Howlett, of Earlham, and sentenced to be transported for 7 years ... Samuel Smith, junior ... was acquitted.

From 'Samuel Smith, alias Cooper's' subsequent declared ages, and if he was one of the defendants in the case in Norwich, he would have been Smith junior; the modus operandi was identical to his subsequent history. There is no record of Smith senior's time either on the hulks or in Australia so what became of him is unknown. However later in the same year, in the Quarter Sessions held at Colchester on 5 October 1801, Samuel Smith of Polstead was found guilty of stealing six pigs, the property of Revd William Ward of Mile End, near Colchester.[1] One of the witnesses against Smith was John Richardson also of Polstead. Smith was sentenced to be transported for seven years 'beyond the seas'.[2]

Samuel Smith was sent to the prison hulk *Prudentia*, moored at Woolwich. The *Prudentia* records, in 1803, give his age as 25. Those sentenced to transportation were mustered in the hulks and employed in 'Hard Labour in raising sand, soil, and gravel from ... the River Thames' while they awaited a ship to take them to Australia. However, the law allowed the prisoners to serve their sentence on the hulks, and this is what Samuel Smith did, escaping actual transportation.[3] He was lucky; the colony in New South Wales was barely 13 years old and life there was very tough – for the transportees as well as the authorities guarding them. On average fewer than 300 convicts were transported each year of Smith's incarceration; the Napoleonic War had broken out in earnest in 1803, and vessels were scarce. Smith was released from the *Prudentia* exactly seven years after his conviction, on 5 October 1808.

Of what he did for the next six years there is no reliable record, but in 1814, during the Essex summer assizes at Chelmsford, the *Chelmsford Chronicle* reported that on 12 March of that year Samuel Smith and Thomas Butterworth were seen driving away four pigs and one hog, value thirteen pounds, the property of Zacharia Piggot and his son.[4] Smith and Butterworth were unable to give a good account of themselves or how they became possessed of the animals and on 27 July 1814, both were sentenced to seven years' transportation.

In the first instance, Smith, now aged 34, was sent to *Captivity*, a hulk moored at Portsmouth.[5] On 23 March 1815, along with 300 other prisoners, he was transferred to the *Baring* which left for New South Wales on 20 April, arriving in Sydney, via Madeira and Rio de Janeiro on 7 September.[87] He was assigned to work for Mr Throsby. Charles Throsby was an 'explorer, grazier, magistrate, member of the upper house and [sometime] surgeon'.[7] Among other things he built Glenfield in Liverpool, now a suburb of Sydney, and it was probably there that Smith was sent as an assigned worker in 1815. He was still there in 1816 and 1817 but on 3 November 1817, he was convicted by Mr Thomas Moore, JP, and sent to Newcastle for one year.

Newcastle was a penal colony where the most difficult prisoners were sent. It was seventy miles north of Sydney and those sent there were subjected to the hard labour of mining coal, cutting trees or lime-burning to make mortar. The work was exhausting, the weather was either unbearably hot or too cold and the environment, with poisonous snakes, 'sandflies, mosquitoes, cholera and dysentery' was highly unpleasant.[8]

Added to that Smith was surrounded by 550 of 'the most turbulent and refractory characters' in New South Wales. The nature of his offence was not recorded, but the contemporary newspapers reported that various other offenders had been sentenced to two years in Newcastle for breaking into a store, three years for stealing a pair of boots and three and seven years respectively for house-breaking. Smith was probably convicted of petty thieving of some description.

It is a measure of Samuel Smith's resilience, or the fact that he was just the type to fit in at Newcastle rather well, that after a year he was back in the Sydney area, assigned to work for Mr Bayly. Bayly was very probably Nicholas Bayly, who owned a thousand acres at Cambramatta, Bayly Park, just north of Liverpool.[9] Two years later, in 1820, Smith was back working for Mr Throsby again and in 1821 he was assigned to Thomas Moore – the magistrate who had sent him to Newcastle; Moore also had an estate in Liverpool.[10] It is interesting to note that in the convict records of Samuel Smith after he returned from Newcastle, his term of transportation was given as life. This must have been incorrect, because he obtained a certificate of his term of transportation having been completed in August 1823.[11] He had been a prisoner for just over nine years, which amounts to seven years in New South Wales, one year in Newcastle and 13 months between date of sentence and arrival in Australia.

In 1826, seventy-two former convicts, 'seven percent of those becoming free to do so' left New South Wales, most of them, presumably, for England.[12] The cost of a steerage ticket from London to Australia in the ship *Berwick* was thirty-five guineas – thirty-six pounds fifteen shillings, equivalent to more than £1,500 today.[13] As an assigned convict, Smith would have had to have worked for ten hours per day, Monday to Friday and six hours on Saturday, but the rest of the time was his own. If he chose to work 'the full day' for his master, or sell his labour elsewhere, the surplus time entitled him to a shilling a day, around eighteen pounds a year.[14] If he spent no money at all – since he was fed by his master – he could have saved more than £100 during his seven-year term.

Thus in August 1823, Samuel Smith, ex pig-thief, ex Newcastle detainee, twice sentenced to be transported, advertised in the *Sydney Gazette and New South Wales Advertiser* that he was leaving the colony on the *Berwick*, and 'request[ed] claims to be presented.'[15] It was normal practice for those departing to make such a declaration. He could have paid for his passage with savings and the sale of his land grant of thirty acres (given to those who had completed their term of transportation). Possibly he stole the cost of a ticket or won it gambling. He may have worked his passage, although he knew nothing of sailing. *Berwick*, a 426 ton three-masted ship had arrived in Hobart in June 1823,

> with a very great number of passengers on board ... after
> a long and tedious passage of six months from England.

That the passage was long and tedious was confirmed when several of the passengers sued the skipper, Captain Jeffery, for the poor conditions on board.[9] *Berwick* arrived in Sydney in August, and spent four months unloading and then loading a cargo. In January 1824, she sailed for England via the Cape of Good Hope. She arrived in Portsmouth on Sunday 11 July 1824.[16]

But Smith was a confirmed and multiple time-serving recidivist. Perhaps he just could not help himself or he knew no other way of making a living, but barely three-and-a-half years later he was apprehended once more and charged with stealing an ass. The Lent Assizes at Chelmsford in March 1828 found him guilty of stealing the animal from Revd P Wright of Marks Tey. This time, Samuel Smith was sentenced to be transported for life.[17] He was sent to the hulk *Leviathan* moored at Portsmouth, where it was noted on the records that he had previously been convicted of a felony. It was while he was there that he was questioned about his knowledge of Maria Martin's murder. On 26 August 1828 he shipped out on the *Royal George*, bound once more for New South Wales.

The record of his presence on the *Royal George* is most illuminating, and provides much of the evidence of his criminal career. His name was given as Samuel Smith alias Cooper, his age was 55 and he was '5 feet 4½ inches tall', with a ruddy complexion and brown-grey hair. It notes his occupation as 'farmer's man and shepherd', and that he was 'Here formerly as Samuel Smith in *Baring*, went home in the *Berwick*'. The *Royal George*, skippered by Captain Embleton, and carrying 158 male prisoners guarded by thirty men of the sixty-third regiment, arrived in Sydney on Christmas Eve 1828.[18] And Samuel Smith, who must have known his way around by this time, was assigned once more to Glenfield and Charles Throsby. But it was Charles Throsby junior, Charles Throsby's nephew, who was his new master. Charles Throsby senior had committed suicide about six months before Smith arrived.

Smith managed to stay out of trouble for the next eight years, because in February 1837, he was granted his Ticket of Leave. The Ticket of Leave, a type of parole, allowed him to work on his own account but only within the district of Bong Bong, an area some miles south-west of Sydney, where the parole had been granted. All was apparently well for the next nine years, but in 1846, the *Sydney Morning Herald* reported a trial that had taken place at the Berrima Circuit Court on 14 September:[19]

> Samuel Smith was indicted for having, at Wombat Brush, on 20th June 1845, assaulted and violated one Emma Fletcher alias Ridgeway.[20]

Smith pleaded not guilty and was 'defended by Mr Sutton', who abandoned the case because Smith insisted on cross-examining the witness himself. To quote from the newspaper report:

The prisoner was an old man of eighty, who was in the service of Mrs Proctor at Wombat Brush, and the girl he was said to have abused was an orphan, apprenticed to that person. The girl was apparently twelve years old, but there was no tangible proof of her age. The girl swore positively to a criminal connection with the prisoner, which appeared to be of some standing.

The jury found Smith guilty of common assault, and he was sentenced to two years in Sydney Gaol. His Ticket of Leave was cancelled.[21]

What happened to Samuel Smith after this is impossible to say. On his release from gaol in September 1848 he would have had to have returned to assigned labour, although there is no record of that. Whether he was as old as 80 at the time of his trial is a moot point; he was at least 70, and his own physical labour was all he had to survive on. It seems unlikely that he would have lived for much longer.

Samuel Smith's sobriquet 'Beauty' has never been explained anywhere. Possibly he was a handsome man; more likely it was an ironic title due to a disfiguring scar or an unfortunate appearance. However, it has been pointed out that in the Suffolk accent, 'Beauty' would have been pronounced booʔy, where 'ʔ' is the glottal stop. 'Beauty' and 'booty' would have sounded the same, and one possible hypothesis for the origin of 'Beauty' Smith's name is that it was actually 'booty', as in 'valuable stolen goods'. This would make sense in the context of his profession as an animal thief, the stolen animals being his valuable booty. Nevertheless regardless of what he looked like, given his documented history both before and after the Maria Martin affair, was he involved in her murder? There is no evidence to connect him to the murder other than the fact of his acquaintance with William Corder when they allegedly conspired in the pig stealing. Donald McCormick's claims that Smith confessed to Thomas Griffiths Wainewright, the artist and poisoner who had been transported for life to Van Diemen's Land* in 1837, that he had stabbed Maria Martin in the Red Barn have been shown to be spurious. The two men could never have met in Australia.†

From what is now known of Samuel Smith's career *before* the Red Barn murder he certainly was a 'notorious thief ... and desperado' as J Curtis described him, and he had already been sentenced to be transported twice as was claimed. Apart from a number of undocumented short terms in gaol, he had spent seven years on the prison hulks in Woolwich, seven years in New South Wales as a transportee, a year in the strict penal colony in Newcastle and the best part of a year at sea going to and coming from Australia. But before the much later episode with the 12-year-old girl, he had never been convicted of any violent crime.

---

\* *Van Diemen's Land* is the old name for Tasmania.
† See Appendix 4.

## Appendix 2 – John Corder, Newsagent and Bookseller of Colchester

William Corder's wife Mary was pregnant at the time of his trial, and their child, John, was born in November 1828 at his grandmother's house in Polstead three months after his father had been executed. John Corder did not die in infancy as has been claimed elsewhere, but he was born with a withered arm, and some reports suggested that he was mentally handicapped. In fact it seems that not only was he able to work, but he was, for a time, a successful businessman.

In the 1851 census, at the age of 21, Corder was registered as a Newsagent, head of the household, living on his own at North Street, Colchester; the following year he married Mary Ann Warren with whom he subsequently had six children.[1] John Corder had certainly effected a remarkable transformation; in 1847, his mother Mary Corder was reported to be poverty-stricken and in deep distress, and John was 'deficient in intellect' and unable to work. His disability may well have been exaggerated in order to improve his mother's chances of assistance, but how he had acquired the capital to set up as a businessman in his own right is a mystery. Evidently business was good, because he was a registered voter in the 1857 parliamentary election, voting for the winning candidate, John Gurdon Rebow; in order to vote, the property Corder occupied had to be worth at least ten pounds per year.[2]

In 1858, Corder was elected a member of the Colchester Property Protection Society, suggesting that at the age of 30 he already had some property to protect.[3] In 1860, he advertised in the *Essex Standard* that he would be shortly supplying the 'London Penny Papers', *The Standard*, *Telegraph* and *Star*, at '6s 6d per Quarter, paid in advance'; furthermore, he had two shops, 111 High Street and 43 North Hill.[4] In December 1860 he was listed as one of the Colchester tradesmen closing on

Christmas Eve, as well as Christmas Day, to allow 'those in our employ' to enjoy two days' Christmas Holiday.[5] The 1861 census showed him living at North Hill with his wife and four children and employing a man and two boys.

During the run-up to Christmas 1864, Corder paid for several large notices in the *Essex Standard* advertising books, Christmas cards, almanacs and the *Illustrated London News*.[6] Each insertion was in the centre of the front page, two columns wide and around thirty lines high. He expanded into printing and started tendering for council business, but by 1868 he had started to overreach himself; his obituary suggests that legal costs might have been responsible for his financial difficulties. In October of that year there was a sale of bankrupt stock consisting of his printing presses and type.[7] Corder survived and continued with his shop in the High Street; in the 1871 census he was still there, now employing a man and three boys.

Things did not improve; in 1874, John Corder was again bankrupt.[8] Apparently he was able to keep trading, since he continued to be described as a bookseller in the various court actions which from this point became more frequent. In 1875, he figured in an extraordinary series of hearings at Boxford in Suffolk. Three Polstead farm labourers, acting under Corder's instructions, were charged with having 'committed damage to the extent of 50s', by cutting some unripe barley from a field belonging to Mr Edward Parson, a farmer of Stoke-by-Nayland.[9] The newspaper report was entitled 'Extraordinary Claim to Landed Property in Suffolk'. Corder had been causing a nuisance in the area putting up placards, and at one point occupying a cottage. The hearing descended into farce, with one of the farm-workers claiming that he was 'as innocent as a sucking duck', Corder interrupting the proceedings and both prosecution and defence solicitors as well as the magistrates apparently enjoying the fun. The farmer, Edward Parson, said at one point that during an argument with Corder, he had told him that he had seen his father hanged... The action cost

Corder '£4 9s 6d' in a fine, damages and costs, and this was paid the same day. Later in the week he was again before the Boxford magistrates to answer a charge of assault along with two soldiers he had recruited from the Colchester barracks to eject one William Scott from a cottage on the disputed land. This time, the magistrates were not amused; the chairman declared:

> [they] were satisfied, from Corder's repeated appearances before them, that any leniency shown to him would be misplaced

He was sentenced to one month's hard labour.[10] Four years later, in 1879, he was again in court accused of having stolen a musical box. It appeared that a joke had been played on him; someone told him he had won it in a draw, and he went and took it while the owner was away from his shop with only a boy left in charge. Once more the proceedings were accompanied by laughter, Corder evidently being regarded as a 'character'. The verdict went against him, and he had to pay expenses and return the musical box or pay twenty pounds in lieu.[11] He continued to make court appearances in the following years; three times for being drunk and disorderly, once for non-payment of the water rate and once for failing to quit rented premises. Sometime after December 1886 he was committed to the Essex lunatic asylum at South Weald where he died, 'after a long affliction', in 1892. The *Essex County Standard* printed an obituary on 22 October 1892:

> The death is announced of Mr John Corder, who at one time was somewhat of a public character in Colchester. Although suffering from a physical infirmity, he was a man of great energy, and some years ago was practically the "only newsagent" in town, and did excellent business. He, however, like many another, fancied he had "rights" in some landed property, and wasted a good deal of

time, substance, and we believe, for a short time, his liberty in his endeavours to enforce these "rights". He was unsuccessful, and as he refused to pay the costs he found himself more than once in the hands of the bailiffs … John Corder passed through many vicissitudes … and finally lost his reason. He was an inmate of Brentwood Asylum, where he died on October 17, in the 64th year of his age.

This not unsympathetic portrait of John Corder makes no reference to his main claim to fame, which from the press report of the barley-cutting in Stoke-by-Nayland, must have been generally known. There can be no doubt that he had been steeped in the injustice of his position by his mother, in having been deprived, as she saw it, of his father's inheritance.

Corder's wife, Mary, carried on the newsagent's business in Colchester for a while with their son John working as her assistant but evidently he was not the businessman his father was. His mother died in 1908, and in the 1911 census he is recorded as a wine-merchant's porter. John Corder junior had five siblings, of which three grew to adulthood, but only his youngest sister married. She however had at least five children, four boys and a girl, and it is, therefore, entirely possible that there are persons alive today directly descended from William Corder of Polstead.

## *Appendix 3 – A Note on Sources*

Pretty well all that is known about the Red Barn affair is derived from just four sources. Since one of these is a sermon by a dissenting minister preaching shortly after William Corder's execution, and another one is the press, the reliability of some of the information is justifiably questionable.

Most contemporary information comes from a minutely detailed book written by 'J Curtis' and published in 1828, shortly after William Corder was hanged.[1] A number of writers have christened him 'James' Curtis, which may have been his name, and it has also been claimed that he was the court reporter for *The Times*. But all that is actually known about him comes from an account by James Grant in *The Great Metropolis*, and Grant consistently refers to him as 'J' Curtis or Mr Curtis.[2] Grant was a newspaper editor and historian; he worked variously for *The Standard*, the *Morning Chronicle* and the *Morning Advertiser*.[3] In the chapter on the Old Bailey in *The Great Metropolis*, Grant describes Curtis as an eccentric character who was there constantly. Curtis was an 'honest, kind-hearted [and] inoffensive' shorthand writer, who took down 'for his own special amusement' every case that came before the New Court.* For some reason he had a horror of the Old Court, which he never attended. Curtis rose early; he regarded four o'clock as a late hour, and apart from attending the Old Bailey, he was fond of walking. Thinking nothing of walking fifty miles in a day, he claimed to have walked, in all, the circumference of the world three or four times. His real specialization though was executions and 'the society of persons sentenced to death'. By his own admission he had been

---

* The written account of the witness evidence in Curtis's book is sufficiently different from that in *The Times* – or any of the other press reports – that this statement is probably true: Curtis did it for his own amusement. There was, in any case, a glaring error in *The Times* account relating to Thomas Martin's mole-spike, which is not repeated by Curtis or anywhere else.

present at every execution in the metropolis and its immediate neighbourhood, for the last quarter of a century.

It was said that he had walked 29 miles from London to Chelmsford before breakfast to be present at the execution of Captain Moir. He was a regular visitor to Newgate,

> [spending] many hours in their gloomy cells, with the leading men who have been executed in London during that time.

He did the same, it was said, with William Corder:

> he contracted a warm friendship; sleeping, I think he has told me, repeatedly on the same bed

As soon as the murder had been discovered,

> [Curtis] hastened ... to the scene, and there remained until the execution of William Corder, making a period of several weeks. He afterwards wrote "Memoirs of Corder" ... published by the present Lord Mayor, then Mr Kelly

Nothing pleased Curtis more than being called Corder's biographer. He did apparently have a sinister demeanour, and was once arrested at Dover on suspicion of being a spy. Moreover, when he tried to take a room at an inn in Chelmsford for Captain Moir's execution, he was refused entry because they thought he was the hangman.

While chronicling the Red Barn murder not only did Curtis share William Corder's bed, he also 'accompanied Corder to his trial, and stood up close to him all the time the trial lasted.' He did this to the extent that a portraitist sent from Ipswich to take Corder's likeness for a newspaper, mistook Curtis for Corder, recorded his portrait, and sent it to the newspaper which duly published it, to the great amusement of Curtis himself.[*] All of which means that J Curtis's account of the Red Barn affair is about as first hand as it is possible to have been, although he was not an objective observer; he never missed an opportunity to enthuse on the monstrosity of one or other of Corder's actions. He also padded out his account with anecdotes, details of sermons and other ephemera, some of them of doubtful relevance, possibly in order to make up his quota of words for the initial publication in parts.[†] There are mistakes and inconsistencies in the book, and in the preface, Curtis apologized to his readers for the various 'errors', which resulted from the instalments being printed and published in London, while he was 'seventy miles' away (in Polstead and Bury) with no opportunity to review the proofs. Nevertheless, the book is exhaustive in the detail provided and serves as a very useful document, effectively a primary source of information about all aspects of the murder; this new investigation relies heavily on Curtis's work. Where a fact has not been explicitly referenced, it usually derives from him.

At this point mention should be made of the spelling of Maria Martin's name, which in all published literature about the affair, until quite recently, is given as *Marten*. The parish records of her father's birth, his two marriages, Maria's birth, that of her brother and sisters, the births of Maria's children, and the registration of her burial all state, without exception, that the surname was *Martin*. The extensive Prosecution Brief for William Corder's trial spelled Maria's surname, and that of her family, *Martin*, and when Maria's father was recorded

---

[*] This may have been the *Bury and Suffolk Herald* of 13 August 1828. A silhouette in profile published on the front page purports to be Corder; 'we can assure our readers [that this is] the best Likeness of Corder yet published.' Since only a full-face portrait of Curtis exists, it is difficult to be sure that it's him. One thing is clear though, the silhouette looks nothing like the other pictures of William Corder.

[†] James Grant reported that instalments of Curtis's work were published in 'sixpenny numbers'.

in the 1851 census at the age of 80, his name was given as Thomas *Martin*.

How did the mistake arise? The original story broke on 23 April, St George's Day, 1828. The story in *The Times*, repeated word for word in *The Standard*, recorded Maria's name correctly as *Martin*. On the same day the *Suffolk Herald*, reported the murder, spelling Maria's name *Marten*. The following day, *The Times* ran a story, 'Murder at Polstead', where again her name was given as Maria *Martin* and the *Morning Chronicle* reproducing the story from the *Suffolk Herald*, quoted her name as *Marten*. On Saturday 26 April, *The Times* ran a two column story on the case referring to both Maria *Marten* and Maria *Martin* in the same piece. Thereafter, she was referred to consistently as Maria *Marten*.

The error may have been compounded by the coroner's court. During the hearing on 25 April when many newspaper reporters were present, the coroner told them that they were not allowed to take notes during the proceedings, fearing that publication of the evidence before the presumed trial could prejudice the outcome. Possibly the misspelling was a piece of sensationalist journalism. *Martin* is a common name; *Marten* is quite rare. Perhaps a newspaperman, keen to generate some cachet to the story, either accidentally or deliberately spelled the name Marten and it stuck.

One further note: Maria's first name would have been pronounced in the old English way, "Mar-eye-a", as in 'Black Maria', not as in romance languages "Mar-ee-a".[4]

The second source of material, and probably the most reliable, is the Prosecution Brief alluded to above. It consists of two copies, each one thirty pages long, with margin notes used by counsel to construct their case.[5] It summarizes all information directly relevant to the affair and also includes the evidence given at the inquest, as well as sworn statements made to the coroner after the inquest. As mentioned, the coroner had not allowed the newspaper reporters to make notes, so the detailed inquest evidence is known only from this document.

The third source is the press. The press interest in the Red Barn affair was phenomenal. Curtis reported that there were between twelve and fifteen reporters present at the inquest into the death of Maria Martin. Everything to do with the murder was reported at length and with relish. There were frequent errors of fact and corrections to previous stories and some of the published tittle-tattle is highly questionable. It is, nevertheless, possible to navigate through the many yards of newsprint and piece together a coherent account of events. Several newspapers including *The Standard*, the *Morning Chronicle*, *The Times* and the *Sunday Times* had detailed accounts of the trial, and these, cross-checked with each other for detail, provide much of the information about the background to the case, the trial itself, the execution and the aftermath.

The last direct source of information is a published sermon by one Charles Hyatt.[6] Hyatt was a minister at the Ebenezer Chapel at Shadwell on the Ratcliff Highway in East London. The Ratcliff Highway was the scene seventeen years earlier of a series of horrific murders. Shadwell was a place of docks and ships, dockworkers and sailors. There must have been a surfeit of sin in such a place, because the area was peppered with churches – three others within a stone's throw of Hyatt's chapel. The area suited Hyatt, because sin was his speciality.

On Sunday 17 August 1828, six days after William Corder was executed, Charles Hyatt preached a sermon, *The Sinner Detected*, near the Red Barn, and also later in the meeting-house at Boxford, a parish adjacent to Polstead. His reasons for 'noticing' the Red Barn affair were that his son-in-law was a minister at Boxford, Corder having attended this ministry at one point, and Charles Hyatt himself had a 'slight personal knowledge' of Corder – he had met him once. Mostly though, it enabled Hyatt to give full vent to his pontificating, sanctimonious, self-righteous piety. He was so pleased with the sermon, that five days later he had it published. Nevertheless, relieved of cant, his piece does have some claim to authority. Hyatt said that he would relate facts:

> which I have received from persons who at some time of his life associated with Corder; and from others that well knew his character, and relying on their veracity I pledge my word for the correctness of the account.

Since, unlike Curtis, Hyatt did have personal connections in the Polstead area, his testimony is also likely to have an element of authenticity. His account is used, together with Curtis's book, to provide much of the background to the lives of Maria Martin and William Corder.

## *Appendix 4 – Previously Published Material*

In the Introduction, it was mentioned that this author expected the Red Barn affair to have been extensively documented, with very little, if anything, needing to be added. For several months the various books that had been published were consulted, and a little research was carried out at the Bury St Edmunds Record Office. Using the substantial records now available concerning transportation to Australia, the progress to that country and back by the character Samuel 'Beauty' Smith was able to be charted. Books by McCormick, 1967, and Haining, 1992, made much of Smith's alleged involvement in the Red Barn murder – Haining reproducing much of what McCormick had claimed in his book. But there were issues with references; Haining had none and several of McCormick's were untraceable. McCormick's findings though were sensational and many of these were treated as fact by Haining.

Then came the breakthrough: McCormick had claimed that Beauty Smith, in Australia, had confessed to another criminal, Thomas Griffiths Wainewright, that he had stabbed Maria Martin in the Red Barn. Wainewright had also been transported, and allegedly had known William Corder in London. The records show, however, that while Smith had been sent to the Sydney area in New South Wales, Wainewright was sent to Van Diemen's Land. It was, therefore, impossible for them ever to have met in Australia. Further discrepancies emerged, and since two of the accounts of the Red Barn affair published after McCormick both refer to his book, it was clear that a complete reinvestigation into the original murder, and what has been written about it since, was appropriate. This review considers the nonfiction books published since 1948 (of which this writer is aware) entirely devoted to the Red Barn murder.

### The MacKenzie reprint of J Curtis's book, 'An Authentic and Faithful History...' 1948[1]

This is an edited reprint of the book by J Curtis, with an epilogue written by Jeanne and Norman MacKenzie. They refer to Curtis as 'unctuous and indefatigable', commenting on his

> disregard for order and his careless appearance ... presented to his public draped in sermons, furbished with irrelevant anecdotes

This resulted, they said, from his publisher, Thomas Kelly, pressing him for 'fresh instalments of a story' which were 'sold as fast as the printers could produce the sheets.' The MacKenzies, not short of an unctuous turn of phrase themselves, removed some of Curtis's more 'irrelevant anecdotes' and ordered his material chronologically. They related how a number of books on the Red Barn murder at the British Museum, including Curtis's, were destroyed during the bombing in World War II; a copy of the Curtis book was found by them in a Canterbury bookshop and this was used as the basis for the reprint. They suggested that similarities in the reports of Corder's trial in Curtis's book and *The Times*, pointed to him being a reporter for that newspaper. They also claimed that John Orridge, the governor at Bury St Edmunds Gaol who supervised Corder's execution, invented the treadmill as used for prison discipline. In a House of Commons report in 1835, Orridge is quoted as saying: 'the first tread-wheel that was erected under my superintendence originated with an idea of my own.'[2] Certainly the first treadmill used in prison was at Bury, although the design is attributed to Sir William Cubitt.[3]

### *The True Story of Maria Marten,*
### Gibbs and Maltby, 1949[4]

Herbert Maltby was the curator of the Moyses Hall Museum in Bury St Edmunds where most memorabilia of the Red Barn murder reside.[5] It is clear from reading Gibbs and Maltby's account that they drew heavily from Curtis's book, and seem to have been the first to call him *James* Curtis. Their book relates the story of Maria Martin in narrative form taking a number of minor liberties with the facts as known. For example, following her mother's death when she was called home to look after her father and younger siblings:

> the only discordant notes in the family life were quarrels between Maria and Ann, a younger sister, who was inclined to resent Maria's undoubted authority in the home.

Then following her 'escapades' with various men:

> Within a few months she had changed from a quiet domesticated girl to a vivacious and ambitious beauty at the beck and call of all the men in the neighbourhood.

And so on. Gibbs and Maltby's final chapter, *Last Judgement*, deals with the question of Ann Martin's dreams. These were the dreams that led to the discovery of the body. The majority of Polstead people, they said, believe that 'Mrs Marten fabricated her dreams out of sheer spite for Corder.' 'Polstead folk', they claim, maintain that 'anxious to get rid of Maria ... Mrs Marten implanted in his mind the idea of killing Maria.' Furthermore, a few of the villagers believed that Maria was 'killed to prevent her hindering a love affair between Corder and Mrs Marten.'

This is interesting material, until it is realized that the villagers whose opinions were being reported were not the Polstead residents of 1828, but those of 1948. They were the 'older folk in Polstead' having been 'told this story by their grandfathers, who knew William, Maria and Mrs Marten'. Perhaps so, but some of them had probably read Curtis's account of the murder, as well as other accounts of the affair. How reliable and unembellished were their 'memories' likely to have been after 120 years and a separation from the events concerned by at least four generations?

Among the numerous pictures embellishing Gibbs and Maltby's book, is a photograph of a knife or 'sword', supplied by the Moyses Hall Museum.* This is supposedly the weapon found in Corder's possession which was allegedly used to stab Maria Martin. The inquest evidence of Robert Offord, a cutler of Hadleigh (close to Polstead) to whom Corder had taken the sword to be sharpened, was:

> a small sword with a white handle, brass-mounted, with
> a scimitar blade ... twelve to thirteen inches long

The sword was presented in court; Curtis described it as 'about two feet in length', but it was in the shape of an 'imperfect crescent'. The knife shown in the photograph has a dark handle, and under no stretch of the imagination could it be considered to be 'scimitar shaped' or an 'imperfect crescent'. It is clearly a butcher's knife, and has subsequently been withdrawn from the Corder exhibit at the museum.

Nevertheless, these quibbles aside, Gibbs and Maltby's book is a readable narrative and a credible exposition of the facts leading to the trial and execution of William Corder. The book was also the first to suggest a romantic liaison between Corder and Mrs Martin as being a possible explanation for her apparent knowledge of the location of Maria's body, assuming that the story of the dreams is rejected.

---

* A picture of this knife is also shown on the cover of Donald McCormick's book.

### *The Red Barn Mystery*, McCormick, 1967[6]

Donald McCormick was a prolific writer and journalist. He met Ian Fleming during the war, and subsequently published numerous works on espionage under the pen name Richard Deacon. He also wrote a biography of Ian Fleming. McCormick was foreign manager for the *Sunday Times* during the 1960s and early 1970s.[7] A number of his books, described as potboilers in his obituary, were on mysterious events: *The Identity of Jack the Ripper*, *Murder by Witchcraft* and *The Mystery of Lord Kitchener's Death*. To those could be added *The Hell-Fire Club*, published in 1958. It attracted a withering review in *The Times*:

> The kindest thing to say about Mr McCormick's book is that he retells ... the familiar mixture of rumour and speculation that hovers around Sir Francis Dashwood's rococo experiments.

The review continued:

> The trouble is that we know almost nothing first hand, and Mr McCormick ... is clearly torn between a desire to make the most of every exciting rumour and the saner view that there was probably more smoke than fire.

The review finished by commenting on the plentiful 'blunders, misquotations and anachronisms' in the book.[8] However, a far more serious charge than blunders, misquotations and anachronisms, was made by the author Melvin Harris.[9] According to Harris, McCormick's books on Jack the Ripper and Lord Kitchener, published in 1959, contain material blatantly manufactured in order to make a good story. Jeremy Duns has made similar charges against McCormick in respect of his Ian Fleming biography.[10]

The subtitle of *The Red Barn Mystery*, says 'Some new evidence on an old murder', and this new evidence is quite sensational in character. McCormick claimed that the reason

Corder always denied stabbing Maria was that unknown to him, his one-time associate Beauty Smith was hiding in the barn when Corder shot her. Corder left to get a spade thinking Maria was dead, but she came to and Smith stabbed her to put her out of her misery. Furthermore, Smith as well as Corder, was having an affair with Ann Martin (Maria's stepmother); Maria was involved in a conspiracy to burgle the Corders' house; the village girl 'H' with whom Corder was supposed to have had an affair had metamorphosed into 'Hannah Fandango', a Creole involved in local smuggling, and Hannah and Corder were acquainted in London with the painter, writer and 'putative poisoner', Thomas Griffiths Wainewright. For good measure, McCormick also claimed that Corder was being blackmailed by one of them. Wainewright was a well-known and well-documented journalist and artist, who was later transported for life to Van Diemen's Land for poisoning his wife.[11]

These extraordinary revelations emerged as the result of some correspondence McCormick had access to between an actress, Caroline Palmer, and a Mrs Hampson, a friend of hers who lived in Sydney. Caroline Palmer, real name Mrs E T Kemp, had played Maria Martin on the stage and having become obsessed with the case, asked her friend Mrs Hampson if she could track down Beauty Smith in Van Diemen's Land where he too had been transported, and get some background on what had really happened. Mrs Hampson did track down Beauty Smith, now 'older and wiser', and living out his life as a gardener there. Wainewright, who had known Corder in London, acted as go-between.

The problem with this fascinating story is that Beauty Smith had been transported to New South Wales, not Van Diemen's Land. Since both he and Wainewright, who *had* been transported to Van Diemen's Land, had been sent to Australia for life, neither man could have travelled out of their local neighbourhood. Both men were eventually granted a Ticket of Leave, a parole that allowed them an element of freedom and the ability to work on their own accounts. The conditions on the granting of this parole were quite clear: the holder was only allowed to travel within the restricted area where it had been issued. Smith's Ticket of Leave was subsequently cancelled following the assault on the 12-year-old child, but it would have been impossible for him ever to have travelled to Van Diemen's Land. Wainewright's time in Van Diemen's Land is well documented. He never left the island, and died there in 1847. There is, therefore, no way that the two men could ever have met in Australia.[12]

No indication was given in McCormick's book of where the Palmer/Hampson correspondence resided and a search for it has proved to be fruitless. McCormick also cited some correspondence between Caroline Palmer and Mary Borham, William Corder's sister, who 'years after the execution of her brother', found some old diaries of his in which he referred to his acquaintance with Wainewright in London. Caroline Palmer became friends with Mary Borham and corresponded with her 'for a few years'. The difficulty with this revelation is that Mary Borham died in January 1829, less than six months after Corder's execution.[13] The parish records of Polstead record her as having been buried there on 5 January 1829.

McCormick reported that Corder's wife, Mary, gave birth prematurely in Lavenham, and she and the child died within hours of each other.* But *The Standard*, on 26 November 1828, reported the birth which took place in *Polstead* on 16 November at the Corders' house. More importantly, press reports and Chancery records in later years detail legal actions Mrs Corder took against her husband's mother and sister; Mary Corder did not die until 1857 and her son, John Corder, lived until 1892.[14]

It was also claimed by McCormick that Corder's early conquest, H, in Hyatt's sermon, the girl who subsequently

---

* Curtis reported that Mrs Corder had gone to live in Lavenham.

became a London prostitute, was a Creole called Hanna Fandango, while cautioning that that might not have been her real name; he said that she also knew Wainewright in London. Unsurprisingly perhaps, no record of such a person exists, but as mentioned in the chapter on William Corder, one newspaper in reporting Hyatt's sermon did name H. The *Bristol Mercury* of 2 September quoted a story from the *Essex Herald* reporting Hyatt's sermon; in respect of Corder:

> he formed an acquaintance with a girl of very loose character, of the name of Hazell

Hyatt's printed sermon contains the words:

> Even at that tender age, it is well known he became acquainted with a poor girl nearly his own age, of the name of H

Consideration of the context, reveals that 'H' was a surname, not a first name as McCormick had assumed, and evidence from parish records allows H to be identified with a family of the name Hazell living in Polstead. Finally, a newspaper or journal, *Settler's Sentinel*, Sydney, 21 July 1859, was cited in McCormick's references. The National Library of Australia have no record of such a publication ever having existed, nor was there any newspaper or journal with either the name *Settler* or *Sentinel* in the title extant in Sydney at the time.[15]

The only possible conclusion that can be drawn from these findings is that Donald McCormick's book on the Red Barn murder and its sensational revelations, including numerous other lesser details not mentioned here, is worthless as an account of historical fact.

### *Maria Marten, The Murder in the Red Barn,* Haining, 1992[16]

Peter Haining was an experienced journalist with over fifty books to his credit, but this one does not start well. The front cover states: 'a reinvestigation of the famous Victorian crime'. Someone might have pointed out to Haining, or indeed his editor, that Queen Victoria did not accede to the throne until ten years after Maria Martin had died, but this is a minor criticism of a book whose contents entirely fail to live up to the claim on the cover. On page 30, after debunking one of the myths associated with the story, that being that Corder was the Martins' ruthless landlord and Maria sacrificed herself for her father's sake, Haining wrote in respect of the Red Barn affair:

> The facts and the fiction seemed to have become so entwined and confused over the years, that no simple version of the events that one turned to told the same story.

Quite so, but then Haining proceeded to add several further layers of obfuscation to the affair, the most egregious of which was to quote freely from a *fictional* account of the murder by William Maginn called *The Red Barn*.[17] He justified this by saying:

> it seems evident that [Maginn] must have obtained considerable 'inside' knowledge of the case before he wrote the book.

Haining pointed out that Maginn's book was first published in 1828, the year of the murder and Haining had access to a 'rare' first edition, rather than the 1831 edition which he claimed was generally thought to be the first publication date.* At the time Maginn's book was published he was a hack journalist

---

* The British Library lists the first publication date as 1828.

'Scribbling in London'. In 1826 he had been charged with 'a familiar intimacy with all the blackguard publications of the age', having edited the first edition of *John Bull* with a 'forged "wedding night" episode of Byron's burnt memoirs'.* In 1827, Maginn published *Whitehall: or, Days of George IV*, which was a spoof of historical novels.[18] In the first sentence of the preface of his book, *The Red Barn*, he stated:

> The following tale is founded on a fact so recently and so notoriously known ... the circumstance on which our Tale is founded, is as legitimate a basis for a novel as any other

He went on to say:

> With the exception of the criminal, his victim, his crime, and those who are not within the range of painful allusion, the characters and adventures in this Novel are purely imaginary ... actual facts have been studiously disregarded, excepting where they were absolutely necessary to the development of the plot.

There can be little doubt, *The Red Barn* is the work of a Grub-Street author struggling to make money from his writing, and finding material and inspiration from wherever he could. A reliable account of historical accuracy it is not, except in the account it has right at the end of the book, after the novel has ended, of the actual murder of Maria Martin and Corder's arrest, trial and execution. This account is drawn from press reports, and completed with copies of the letters written to Corder in response to his advertisements for a wife. Nevertheless, Haining was convinced of Maginn's 'considerable inside knowledge', and reproduced, as fact, items from the book. For example, on page 34, he wrote:

---

* In 1824, John Murray, the publisher, had burnt Byron's memoirs because they were too scandalous; John Samuel Murray, 1778 – 1843, *ODNB*.

> according to a local story, [Maria] had had her future
> read when she was sixteen by a gypsy fortune-teller

This was straight from Maginn's book, although it was also mentioned by McCormick, and was embellished by an illustration which Haining reproduced.[19] But the very worst example of Haining's deliberate confusion of fact and fiction occurs on Page 43. He reproduced an illustration from Maginn's book showing characters from that fictional account, including the Corder character, whose name was Barnard, gambling in London. Haining named them Corder, Beauty Smith and Thomas Griffiths Wainewright. He thus conflated Maginn's fiction with McCormick's account, purportedly fact, and represented the whole thing as fact. Elsewhere, he quoted freely and extensively from McCormick's book, reproducing many of his spurious claims. Not content with wilfully muddling fact and fantasy, Haining introduced an entirely new and original strain of mythology into the Red Barn affair from a misreading of the *Sunday Times* report of the trial and an elementary failure to cross-check his 'remarkable' finding with other newspapers. In Curtis's account of the trial, he reported Thomas Martin's evidence regarding the initial discovery of his daughter's body:

> The body was ... not stretched out. The hole appeared
> to be about three feet or three feet and a half long. The
> legs were drawn up, and the head bent down. I put my
> mole-spike near the hip-bone; the spike is about as thick
> as my little finger.[20]

The report from the *Morning Chronicle*:

> I poked down the earth with the handle of the rake and
> with a mole spike that I had with me; we spiked down
> those two things, both of us, and turned up something
> that was black, and pieces of something like flesh stuck

> to the spike, and I smelled it, and thought it was flesh ...
> the mole spike was iron, about a foot long, and round[21]

*The Standard*, reporting the same evidence:

> [He] poked down with the handle of a rake and mole-spike he had with him ... something that appeared to be flesh stuck to the pike [sic] ... The mole-spike is round, and sharp at one end.[22]

The meaning is clear and unambiguous: Thomas Martin probed the ground with his mole-spike which was round, about a foot long and made of iron; the sharp end was the thickness of his little finger. Haining quoted from the *Sunday Times* report of the same evidence:

> the body was lying down, but not stretched out; it was about three feet and a half; the legs were bent up, and the head was bent down a little in the earth. A spike was driven into the body about the hip bone; the smallest end of the spike was about the size of my little finger[23]

Except that the actual passage from the newspaper is:

> the body was lying down, but not stretched out; it was about three feet and a half; the legs were bent up, and the head was bent down a little in the earth; the spike was driven into the body about the hip bone; the smallest end of the spike was about the size of my little finger[24]

Haining had misread the quotation; he replaced the definite article 'the', clearly referring to Thomas Martin's mole-spike, with the indefinite article 'a', 'A spike'; he also replaced the semicolon with a full stop. He then started talking about vampirism and Maria Martin being 'pinned to the earth' with the non-existent spike. He even reproduced a photograph apparently of the staked skeleton of a suspected witch. He commented:

the strangeness of this discovery still puzzles me, and I am surprised that no-one else appears to have noticed or commented upon it.[25]

Intriguingly, Haining may have also read the account in *The Times* where the reporter apparently made the same mistake that he did:

On that spot he poked down the handle of the rake, and turned up something which was black. On getting further assistance they discovered, a little under the ground, a small sharp iron about a foot long, like a hay spike[26]

Thus was created another myth about Maria Martin's death, a myth that was subsequently repeated by Nessworthy in her book about the case. Peter Haining did not deliberately manufacture evidence to make a good story, but he succeeded in achieving the absolute opposite of his avowed aim, that being to separate clearly fact and fiction in the Red Barn murder. He added several new layers of foolishness to the deliberate muddle already created by Donald McCormick.

### *Murdering Maria*, Nessworthy, 2001[27]

Linda Nessworthy is a distant relation of William Corder, and in 2001 she published an account of the Red Barn affair, *Murdering Maria*. The book includes a genealogy of the Corder family and a previously unpublished defence statement taken from an original handwritten copy by Corder himself. Nessworthy was the first to point out the misspelling of Maria Martin's name. Much more importantly, she found the information allegedly from Mr Orridge, the prison governor, regarding the stab wounds found on Maria's body which was published in the *Sunday Times* after Corder's execution.

There are some errors and omissions in the book, and several of McCormick's various claims are repeated as fact, although more surprising is Nessworthy's presentation of William Corder's defence statement. She has a 'photographed copy' of this document, which is in private hands, and a transcript of it is reproduced verbatim. However, it is quite clearly *not* the statement that was read out by Corder in court, since in Nessworthy's copy of the statement, he says that he and Maria parted company after their argument in the Red Barn and he never saw her again. What Corder actually said, as attested by all the press reports, is that when he left Maria in the barn following the argument, he heard a shot and returned to find her lying on the floor having apparently shot herself with one of his pistols. Naturally, Nessworthy's defence statement is most interesting as an early draft, but it is not the one Corder used in court.

As a member of the Corder family, Linda Nessworthy campaigned, successfully, to have Corder's skeleton removed from The Royal College of Surgeons' Huntarian Museum, and cremated. She also wishes to have Corder's grisly remains removed from the Moyses Hall Museum in Bury St Edmunds and likewise laid to rest. These consist of his scalp with an ear still attached, and a copy of Curtis's book bound in Corder's skin. This writer supports her in that endeavour.

### *William Corder and the Red Barn Murder*, McCorristine, 2014[28]

Dr McCorristine's book is part of 'Harnessing the Power of the Criminal Corpse', a project at Leicester University funded by the Wellcome Trust. It is an academic work concerned principally with the aftermath of William Corder's execution, his 'celebrity corpse' and the sociological consequences arising. The book contains some excellent references to material in the press of which this writer was unaware, and recognizes the misspelling of Maria Martin's name. Donald McCormick's so-called 'new evidence' is identified as having been fabricated.

# *References*

## Prologue

1   www.plant-lore.com claims that when the tree collapsed in 1953 it had over 1,400 growth rings. Elsewhere it is stated variously that its girth was either 32 or 36 feet.

2   Harley, Lawrence S, *Polstead Church and Parish*, (Polstead, Polstead Parochial Church Council, 1998).

3   Evans, Eric J, *The Forging of the Modern State* (Harlow, Longman, 1983).

4   *Leicester Chronicle*, 24 December 1830.

## Maria Martin

1   Whitmore, John, *An Address to my Parishioners and Neighbours on the subject of the Murder... By a Suffolk Clergyman* (London, Seely & Son, 1828). The British Library copy of this book, attributed to John Whitmore, has a handwritten note on the flyleaf: 'When this murder was committed, the Revd John Whitmore was Rector of Polstead. It does not clearly appear whether he was the author of this address or not.' The book has virtually no personal details of either Maria Martin or William Corder, which is strange considering that they were members of Whitmore's parish. The author claims that Maria was dismissed from her post with the clergyman at Layham when she was 15 years old, which was long after her mother died, and this conflicts with what Curtis said. On page one, the author comments: 'the subject of this address, has been made known to us through the County Newspapers' which suggests that he had little inside knowledge of events. There is no record of Whitmore visiting William Corder in prison. The author

claims he was present in the chapel attended by Corder just before his execution, and implies from details given, that he was present when Corder was led out to the scaffold. Either Whitmore was not the author, or he was, but he so distanced himself from the scandalous events, apparently offering no comfort or care to those involved, that, other than moralizing, he had no real information to impart on the Red Barn affair.

2   Curtis, J, *An Authentic and Faithful History of the Mysterious Murder of Maria Marten*... (London, Thomas Kelly 1849) 40 et seq. Information on Maria's family and early life is taken generally from Curtis's book together with some basic genealogy of the Martin family derived from the Polstead parish registers.

3   Cunningham, Peter, *Hand-Book of London* (London, John Murray, 1850) 126.

4   Information on Peter Mathews from a variety of sources; for example, Gentleman's Magazine, Aug 1837, 210, Feb 1850, 229, 338. Will of Richard Mathews, 1826, Prerogative Court of Canterbury, National Archives.

5   FL 521/7/35/17 and FL 521/9/2/3, Bury Record Office.

6   Polstead Parish Register of births, Bury Record Office.

**William Corder**

1   Polstead parish register, Bury Record Office.

2   Curtis, op. cit., 70 et seq.

3   *Sunday Times*, 10 August 1828, which may have referenced one of Curtis's 'ephemeral publications'.

4   McCormick, Donald, *The Red Barn Mystery, Some new evidence on an old murder* (London, John Long, 1967) 30.

5   *Colours and Finishes for Historic Buildings*, (Bury St Edmunds, St Edmundsbury Borough Council, November 2007).

6   Cresswell, Julia, *Dictionary of First Names* (London, Bloomsbury, 1990).

7   FL 521/7/35/17 & FL 521/9/2/3, Bury Record Office.

8   Parish records, Bury Record Office.

9   Will of John Corder of Polstead, DAVY 177, 1826, Norfolk Record Office.

**Those Twain**

1   Nessworthy, Linda, *Murdering Maria* (Great Yarmouth, Malinda Publishing, 2001) 65 et seq.

**What William Did Next...**

1   *Leicester Chronicle*, 30 June 1827.

2   Foster, George, *An Accurate Account of the Trial of William Corder*, (London, George Foster, 1828). This book is freely available on *Google Books*; the letters from fifty-three ladies, some representing friends or relatives, one openly suspicious of Corder's motives, but most from young women, 'not handsome' and without the 'power of property' were mostly responding to the advertisement in the *Sunday Times*, where the requirement for 'property' had been omitted.

3   Foster, op. cit.

4   Curtis, op. cit., 256.

5   *Times*, 3 December 1827.

6   *Ipswich Journal*, 3 May 1828.

7   Curtis, op. cit., 223.

8   Curtis, op. cit., 18.

9   McCormick, op. cit., 130.


**A Discovery, an Inquest and an Arrest...**

1   The Proceedings of the Old Bailey online.

2   *Morning Chronicle,* 24 April 1828.

3   Curtis, op. cit., 222.

4   Sir William Rowley, 2nd Bt. (1761 – 1832) of Tendring Hall;
    Member of Parliament for Suffolk.


**Problems with the Prosecution, not to mention the Defence**

1   *Standard*, 4 August 1828.

2   *Observer*, 3 August 1828.


**The Trial**

1   Foss, Edward, *A Biographical Dictionary of the Judges of
    England*, (London, John Murray, 1870).

2   *Times*, 8 August 1828.

3   *Standard*, 8 August 1828.

4   Curtis, op. cit., 109, 178 & 179.

5   *Morning Chronicle*, 8 August 1828.

6   *Times*, 8 August 1828.

7   *Standard*, 8 August 1828.

8    *Standard*, 9 August 1828.

9    Bentley, D J, *English Criminal Justice in the 19th Century*, (London, Hambledon Press, 1998).

10   *Times*, 12 September 1828.

**The Final Act**

1    *Morning Post*, 21 August 1823.

2    *Standard*, 13 August 1828.

3    Curtis, op. cit., 302.

4    Curtis, op. cit., 304.

**Aftermath**

1    Curtis reported that someone who witnessed the hanging attended a performance of Macbeth that evening in a town not far from Bury. When King Duncan said "Is execution done on Cawdor?" the man said: "Yes sir, I saw him hanged this morning; and I'll not answer any more questions about it." The performance was held up for some time with the audience convulsed in laughter.

2    Curtis, op. cit., 307.

3    *Sunday Times*, 17 August 1828.

4    *Bury and Norwich Post*, 20 August 1828.

5    *Bury and Suffolk Herald*, 20 August 1828.

6    *Bury and Suffolk Herald*, 3 September 1828.

7    Curtis, op. cit., 310.

8    Curtis, op. cit., 311.

## Respice

1  *Bath Chronicle*, reported in *Berrow's Worcester Journal*, 25 September 1828.

2  See for example, *Ipswich Journal*, 3 May 1828.

3  *Times*, 26 April 1828.

4  Gibbs, Dorothy, and Maltby, Herbert, *The True Story of Maria Marten*, (Ipswich, East Anglian Magazine, 1949).

5  Curtis, op. cit., 13.

6  1851 Census return for Polstead.

7  Curtis, op. cit., 365.

8  *Ipswich Journal*, 3 May 1828.

9  McCormick, op. cit., 193.

10 *Legal Observer*, Vol 1, No II, Saturday 13 November 1830, 21-22.


## Epilogue

1  Haining, Peter, *Maria Marten, The Murder in the Red Barn*, (Plymouth, Images, 1992) 125.

2  *Morning Chronicle*, 4 September 1828.

3  Harley, Op. Cit.

4  *Standard*, 3 September 1828, reprinted from the *Suffolk Herald.*

5  *Suffolk Herald*, 14 May 1828.

6  C13/1067/21, Chancery Papers, National Archives, Kew.

7  *Essex Standard*, 11 March 1836.

8  *Essex Standard*, 24 September 1841.

9 *Essex Standard*, 29 January 1847.

10 *Essex Standard*, 24 September 1847.

11 *Trewman's Exeter Flying Post*, 23 November 1848.

12 *Essex Standard*, 19 June 1857.

13 Will of Peter Mathews, formerly of Clement's Inn ... late of New Steyne Brighton ... proved in the Principal Registry of Her Majesty's Court of Probate, 30 January 1871.

14 *Morning Chronicle*, 3 April 1845.

## Appendix 1 – Beauty Smith

1 William Ward was eventually appointed bishop of Sodor and Man in 1827, the same year that the Red Barn murder took place.

2 *Bury & Norwich Post*, 14 Oct 1801 and Essex Record Office Quarter Sessions, Sb6/9.

3 Act of Parliament, 1779, 19th Geo. III., cap. 74.

4 *Chelmsford Chronicle*, 5 Aug 1814.

5 HO9; piece 8; Convict Prison Hulks: Registers and Letter Books.

6 HO 10; piece 1/2 Australia Settler and Convict Lists, 1787-1834 and *The Sydney Gazette and New South Wales Advertiser*, 9th September 1815.

7 *Australian Dictionary of Biography* on line.

8 Hughes, Robert, *The Fatal Shore*, (London, Folio Society, 1998) 402.

9 *Australian Dictionary of Biography*, op. cit.

10 *Australian Dictionary of Biography*, op. cit.

11 *Sydney Gazette and New South Wales Advertiser*, 4 September 1823. The newspaper notice is ambiguous; those reported had received either a Ticket of Leave or a Certificate [of completion of sentence]. In view of what happened next, ie. Smith's return to England, it must have been a certificate.

12 Shaw, A G L, *Convicts and the Colonies*, (Melbourne, Melbourne University Press, 1966) 144.

13 *Hobart Town Gazette and Van Diemen's Land Advertiser*, 26 July 1823.

14 Huges, op. cit., P266.

15 *Sydney Gazette and New South Wales Advertiser,* 28 August 1823.

16 Four years later, the ship was wrecked homeward bound from Bombay to London with the loss of the captain, first mate and thirteen crew.

17 *Chelmsford Chronicle*, 14 March 1828.

18 *Sydney Gazette and New South Wales Advertiser,* 26 December 1828.

19 *Sydney Morning Herald*, 13 September, 1846.

20 Wombat Brush, now called Canyon Leigh, is around 80 miles south west of Sydney.

21 It was from details on Smith's ticket of leave, that the man charged with assault on the child was positively identified as Samuel Smith alias Cooper.

## Appendix 2 - John Corder of Colchester

1   *Essex Standard*, 9 July 1852.

2   *Essex Standard*, 24 February 1857.

3  *Essex Standard*, 7 May 1858.

4  *Essex Standard*, 22 June 1860.

5  *Essex Standard*, 19 December 1860.

6  *Essex Standard*, 9 December 1864.

7  *Essex Standard*, 28 October 1868.

8  *Essex Standard*, 5 June 1874.

9  50s = 50 shillings or two pounds ten shillings (20 shillings = one pound). Equivalent to around £125 in 2005 prices.

10 *Essex Standard*, 31 August 1875.

11 *Essex Standard*, 19 July 1879.

### Appendix 3 – A Note on Sources

1  Curtis, op. cit.

2  Grant, James, *The Great Metropolis*, Volume II, Second Series, (London, Saunders and Otley, 1837) 199.

3  *Oxford Dictionary of National Biography, ODNB.*

4  *Oxford English Dictionary, OED.* The phonetic spelling of Maria is 'mə'rʌiə'.

5  Suffolk Summer Assizes 1828. The King ag William Corder for the Wilful Murder of Maria Martin, Brief for the Prosecution, 568/1 & 568/2, Bury St Edmunds Record Office.

6  Hyatt, Charles, *The Sinner Detected*, (London, Westley and Davis, 1828).

## Appendix 4 - Previously Published Material

1   Curtis, J, *An Authentic and Faithful History*... J Curtis, edited by Jeanne and Norman MacKenzie (London, Pilot Press, 1948).

2   *Selection of Reports and Papers of the House of Commons*, Vol 54 Prisons, 6 May 1835, 299.

3   *Remarks upon Prison Discipline*, A Letter addressed to the Lord Lieutenant and Magistrates of the County of Essex from C C Western, Esq. M.P., James Ridgway, London, 1821.

4   Gibbs and Maltby, op.cit.

5   From the St Edmundsbury Chronicle, www.stedmundsburychronicle.co.uk.

6   McCormick, op. cit.

7   *Guardian*, 5 March 1998.

8   *Times*, 10 April 1958.

9   www.casebook.org/dissertations/maybrick_diary/mb-mc.html, Melvin Harris.

10  www.jeremy-duns.com/blog/licence-to-hoax, Jeremy Duns.

11  *ODNB.*

12  See Appendix 1 for full details of Beauty Smith's life.

13  *Bury and Norwich Post*, 28 January 1829.

14  *Essex County Standard*, 22 October 1892.

15  National Library of Australia, NLAref82255, Private communication, 14 March 2014.

16  Haining, op. cit.

17 Maginn, William, *The Red Barn, A Tale, Founded on Fact*, (London, John Bennett, 1831). There is a minor mystery regarding the authorship of this book, published anonymously, but variously attributed to either William Maginn or Robert Huish. The *ODNB* says Maginn may have written the book; the entry for Robert Huish does not mention it. The British Library and Google Books each have virtually identical versions attributed to both authors. Intriguingly, the Google Books version, attributed to William Maginn, Printed for John Bennet, 1831, has 'Robert Huish' written on the title page. The version attributed to Robert Huish, was printed for Knight and Lacey, 1828. The British Library also has a copy of this version. Its copy attributed to Maginn was also published for Knight and Lacey, 1828. Huish did write on historical topics and romances, but his main claim to fame was as an expert apiarist. On balance, Maginn seems the likeliest author, and this has been assumed in the present text.

18 Information on Maginn's life from the *ODNB.*

19 Maginn, op. cit., 11 et. sec. including an illustration.

20 Curtis, op. cit.

21 *Morning Chronicle*, 8 August 1828.

22 *Standard*, 8 August 1828.

23 Haining, op. cit., 67.

24 *Sunday Times*, 8 August 1828.

25 Haining, op. cit., 70.

26 *Times*, 8 August 1828.

27 Nessworthy, op. cit.

28 McCorristine, Shane, *William Corder and the Red Barn Murder*, (Basingstoke, Palgrave Macmillan, 2014).

# Picture credits

Maria Martin, from an image published in J Curtis's book, 1849 edition.

William Corder, Bury St Edmunds Record Office.

William Corder's Death Mask, Norfolk Museums Service (Norwich Castle Museum & Art Gallery).

Thomas and Ann Martin, from images published in J Curtis's book, 1849 edition.

Maria Martin's Cottage, Bury St Edmunds Record Office.

The Corder House, by Bruce Hatton.

The Red Barn, Bury St Edmunds Record Office.

Polstead Tithe map, by kind permission of the Diocese of St Edmundsbury and Ipswich.

The execution of William Corder, from an image published in J Curtis's book, 1849 edition.

Front and back cover, The Red Barn, Bury St Edmunds Record Office.

# *Index*